Special Needs in the Primary School: Identification and Intervention

Special Needs in the Primary School: Identification and Intervention

Lea Pearson
Geoff Lindsay

NFER-NELSON

Published by The NFER-NELSON Publishing Company Ltd.,
Darville House, 2 Oxford Road East,
Windsor, Berkshire SL4 1DF, England

First Published 1986
Reprinted 1986, 1987

Library of Congress Cataloging in Publication data

Pearson, Lea.
  Identification and intervention.

  1.Handicapped children–Education (Elementary)–Great Britain. 2.
Handicapped children–Great Britain–Identification. 3. Handicapped
children–Education–Law and legislation–Great Britain. I. Lindsay, Geoff.
II. Title.
LC4036.G7P43 1986   371.9'0941   86-2435
ISBN 0-7005-1005-2

Photoset by David John (Services) Ltd., Maidenhead

Printed in Great Britain by A. Wheaton & Co., Ltd., Exeter

ISBN 0 7005 1005 2
Code 8197 02 1

Contents

Foreword

The 1981 Education Act requires governors 'to secure that the teachers in the school are aware of the importance of identifying, and providing for those pupils who have special educational needs'. Most teachers are in fact aware of this, but may wonder how it can be achieved. Lea Pearson and Geoff Lindsay are two educational psychologists who have been working on this problem for many years, and in this short book they offer primary schools the outcome of their research and thinking.

There can be few primary schools whose teachers doubt that they have a key role in identifying and meeting the special educational needs of a large proportion of children. As the Fish Report emphasized, this is not a role which is tacked on to the education of a hypothetical group of 'normal' children. On the contrary, it is a direct outcome of teachers' awareness of the structure of the broad curriculum, and of their children's progress through this. Pearson and Lindsay stress throughout their book, that the assessment of children's needs is meaningless if it is separated from attempts to meet their needs. They describe how this is carried out in the context of support services both within the school and outside. Teachers in primary schools have to have a mutually agreed policy and a strategy concerning children with special needs, and the authors break new ground in offering an overview of how this might be achieved.

It is heartening that, at a time when it is so difficult for teachers to feel optimistic about their role, Pearson and Lindsay can point to the positive strategies offered by the new thinking emerging from the education of children with special educational needs.

K. Wedell

Preface

All schools are aware of the 1981 Education Act and of its requirements for a significant proportion of children in ordinary schools with some form of special needs. Some local education authorities are actually asking their schools to produce a framework or policy for special needs. Even when such a request is not being made many teachers are eager to plan their own strategies.

In Part I of this book we have attempted to provide a concise and readable account of the Act and its implications, and of how schools can plan for special needs. We are not recommending any particular model – indeed it would be naive to do so given the enormous variation between schools. We do offer a framework that can accommodate a range of specific approaches that suit individual schools' needs. In Part II we summarize critically some of the specific approaches that are currently popular. This is an unashamedly eclectic range which derives from different models. We are convinced that schools and others involved should evaluate the effectiveness of any approach they adopt. We are not convinced that any one approach has proven superiority. Indeed we are aware of a growing body of educational opinion that suggests that time on task is the main significant predictor of children's progress – what task from what theory is less significant.

We are not uncritical of the Act. We do not see schools as unsophisticated institutions that have been unaware of children's needs until statute drew attention to them. Nor are we unaware of the competing demands that are being made on schools. However, despite decades of joint experience as teachers, researchers and predominantly as educational psychologists we are excited and optimistic about the philosophy of the Warnock Report and the Act, and the specific developments that coincide with these. The

1981 Act, despite its cumbersome procedures, has an implicit vision of a better world, a better deal for the children who are often a nuisance to teachers, a source of anxiety to their parents, and an administrative liability to LEAs. We hope that teachers, psychologists, advisers, administrators, parents, and anyone concerned, share with us this albeit vague notion of equality, opportunity, change and progress – and that we offer some practical advice on translating this into a practical reality.

Lea Pearson
Geoff Lindsay
1986

Part I
General Issues

CHAPTER 1
The Education Act 1981

Previous Legislation

Until the 1981 Education Act became statute in April 1983, the major legislation concerning special education comprised sections of the 1944 Education Act. Of course special education was not discovered in 1944, but dates back to developments in the eighteenth century. These were charitable ventures, providing education or vocational training for the 'deaf and dumb' and the blind. In the nineteenth century such provision grew and extended to the physically handicapped and the 'mentally defective'. By the end of the nineteenth century the first legislation concerning special education in the UK was in existence. The 1870 Elementary Education Act (the Forster Act) and corresponding legislation in Scotland in 1872 established school boards to ensure the provision of elementary education, and subsequent legislation required these boards to provide education for some groups of handicapped children.

The 1902 Education Act replaced school boards with local education authorities. Between 1902 and 1944 a range of developments, usually led by volunteer or charitable groups or individuals took place; the previous piecemeal legislation on special education was consolidated in the 1921 Education Act. In the same period educational psychologists and the child guidance movement appeared. The London County Council appointed Cyril Burt in 1913; by 1939, 22 child guidance clinics were established as part of the school medical service.

The 1944 Education Act (in Scotland a slightly different Act, the 1945 Education (Scotland) Act) was the first British legislation to include special education within the general duties laid down for local education authorities: 'to afford for all pupils opportunities for education offering such variety of instruction and training as may be desirable in view of their different ages, abilities and aptitudes, and of the different periods for which they may be expected to remain at school'. The regulations of the Act defined 11 categories of handicap: blind, partially sighted, deaf, partially deaf, delicate, diabetic, educationally subnormal, epileptic, maladjusted, physically handicapped and those with speech defects. The 1970 Education (Handicapped Children) Act was implemented in April 1971 and added the responsibility for the education of mentally handicapped children who had previously been deemed 'ineducable' and subject to provision by health authorities.

Under the 1944 Act children were ascertained by a medical officer as suffering from a disability of mind or body. Guidance issued by the Ministry of Education (1946) estimated the likely percentage of the different handicapping conditions, and made it plain that many entailed education in a special school. In 1975 a Department of Education and Science circular examined the processes of identification and assessment and provided new forms for the educational, medical and psychological advice. These forms (SE Forms 1–3) were accompanied by a summary form (Form SE4) which was completed in most LEAs by the psychologist. This circular was a significant stage in the changing concept of special education – from a medical to an educational one.

The Warnock Report

The Warnock Committee reported on the education of handicapped children and young persons in 1978. Their report certainly provided the impetus for the 1981 Act, although its findings and recommendations were wider than the Act. The report will soon be ten years old, and it seems unlikely that it has much further potential for directly influencing developments and change. However, many of the Warnock concepts have been absorbed into current educational thinking and it is perhaps still useful to summarize these.

The report views the scope of special educational needs as a continuum, from minor and temporary needs to major and lasting ones. It seeks to establish the concepts of special provision, wherever this is made, as additional or supplementary to general education, not as separate or alternative provision. Consequently all children are seen as having a basic right to education as enshrined in the 1944 Education Act. The old terminology of categories is replaced by one of special need, and learning difficulty becomes a generic term for children with mild, moderate or severe problems. Children from birth to 19 years are covered. The report also estimates that one in five children will have a special need at some stage in their school career, and that one in six will at any given time. While these 'statistics' are much quoted to demonstrate that every teacher and every class have children with special needs, they are based on epidemiological studies that were made before the report. It seems likely that if special needs were defined more precisely than has been done so far, any current survey would indicate even higher figures.

Parents are conceptualized as partners, and at various points in the report their rights, and the improvement in provision that would facilitate their role, are emphasized. For parents of children with special educational needs a 'named person' is suggested who can be their point of contact, friend, or even advocate. While some LEAs have pursued this, many others have not.

The assessment of special needs is seen as a five-stage process – initially the responsibility of the head and the school, secondly involving an advisory 'expert' teacher, thirdly bringing in one or more other visiting professionals, fourthly a multiprofessional assessment, and fifthly a formal assessment of a child's needs. Such assessment is linked to the need for good records at all levels, and to an annual review following the formal assessment of special needs.

The provision for children who have special needs includes special schools, but there are recommendations encouraging these to be similar to and linked with mainstream education. The development of suitable curricula and the training of all teachers are also emphasized, as is the need for greatly improved pre-school and post-school provision. The final chapters consider the arrangements LEAs need to make, the work of other staff in the education, health and social and voluntary services, and their relationships. Finally, the need for research and development locally and nationally is emphasized and the establishment of a national Special Educational Research Group recommended. The implementation of this latter recommendation is favoured by various voluntary and professional groups but to date does not seem likely to be implemented.

The Education Act 1981 and Special Needs

The DES (1980) issued a White Paper entitled *Special Needs in Education* which indicated the government's intention to produce a Bill, and outlined their intention to move from a classification of disability to a concept of special needs. The paper acknowledged that 'in one sense every child's educational needs are "special" because they are peculiar to him, and nearly every child from time to time has difficulties which distinguish him from others'. In that sense the White Paper recognized the continuum of special needs. However, it also emphasized that a new legal framework was required only for the minority whose problems are greater and more persistent. The needs of most children could be met as part of the integral provision that schools make for the whole range of their pupils. It was also suggested that special needs should be a priority area in in-service training, and that authorities would need to provide specialist support services that teachers could draw on freely.

The 1981 Act and subsequent DES circulars (8/81 and 1/83) continue with these predictions in as much as the largest part concerns the small proportion of children who require the protection of a statement. While this book is focused on the wider range of special needs met within the primary school it is perhaps helpful to consider the schools' role with reference to children with statements and this is outlined below.

The Act, as Circular 1/83 outlines, requires school governors and the LEA to ensure that ordinary schools fulfil obligations to identify any children who have special needs and to ensure both that appropriate provision is made, and that such children engage with their peers in the ordinary activities of the school. It is also emphasized in circulars that parents should be involved as partners.

There seems little doubt that the great majority of schools and teachers welcomed the broad Warnock concepts and would like to implement the Act and help children with special needs. There is however a significant gap between such laudable general aims and their practical application at the classroom level. Although 'special needs' has become a common phrase in the educational world, defining such needs so that it is clear which children should receive appropriate provision is problematic.

There seem to be varied approaches which constitute two broad categories of definition. For children put forward for section 5 procedures or the process leading to a statement, the Act refers to 'significantly greater difficulty in learning than the majority of children of his age'. This has a clear implication that some sort of norm-referenced assessment will back up such a definition, that a child has special needs in some fairly absolute sense related to the whole population of children of that age group. A similar definition can extend to any identification of special need – that one should use a test, checklist or screening procedure to check that this is a real problem, one that some notional average child would not have. This is a piece of information that has an instinctive appeal to many people. Teachers feel that some such measure vindicates their concern; parents can understand it, particularly if it is explained to them as an age lag – although he or she is seven, behaviour/concentration/language would be average for a four-year-old.

However, when such a measure does not substantiate a concern which is none the less real, teachers may opt for a relative judgement not comparing to the total population but to other children in the class. Of course the so called 'absolute' judgement is also relative, but relative to a far larger group. Such issues have been debated for years with reference to extra resources or staffing or support services. Should these be available to all schools on the grounds that problems are relative and can be just as difficult to teach in a middle-class school as an inner city one? Should one resource the deprived areas and tell the others that they do not have problems in the same sense?

It seems a sensible debate if one has to allocate limited resources somehow. It seems a silly one with reference to individual children, since one can easily use both definitions or criteria. Neither offers a clear definition of special needs, and since these could be complex or simple, temporary or longer term, to do with specific areas of learning or the general process, or behaviour, or a child's disability or problem, it is perhaps not useful to try to do so. The key concept is educational – not other – needs, so schools need to be reasonably certain that their pupils are functioning within some sort of normal limits, and also to consider clarifying any problems that are apparent to the teacher, and ways of meeting them. It seems quite sensible to say of a child that he or she is low average in a certain area, and that this is in itself a problem if all his or her peers are literally years ahead. Indeed it is probably more reassuring for parents and others than merely stressing what the child cannot do relative to his or her peers without some general context.

Although primary schools are not immune from emotional and behavioural problems, learning difficulties tend to predominate.

The Warnock Report discussed curriculum and provision with reference to special needs seeing special provision as being likely to emphasize access to the curriculum for children with sensory or physical handicaps, a restricted curriculum for children with learning difficulties, or an emphasis on the social structure and emotional climate in which instruction takes place. The DES, in revising Form 7H (the form returned by LEAs describing their special-needs pupils) to fit with the new legislation, specify three sorts of curriculum – ordinary, restricted and developmental. The ordinary curriculum is just that; a restricted curriculum would be for children with moderate learning difficulties whose objectives would be limited and at secondary level might include an older version of aspects of the ordinary junior school curriculum; a developmental curriculum would be for children with severe learning difficulties with an emphasis on language, self-help skills, social competencies and might include substantial programmes leading to mastery of skills that children on an ordinary curriculum would have learned incidentally before starting school.

This distinction has not had much publicity, but it is useful. For some special schools it has highlighted the unrealistic demands to teach all three types in a single class linked by a handicap rather than educational needs. It seems likely that LEAs will move towards either limiting the range of curricular demands made of a particular class or school, or resourcing schools to meet them adequately. For a primary school it is a useful concept, whether a school opts to educate only children who need an ordinary curriculum with some additional help, or whether they opt to offer a restricted alternative, and seek resources to do so.

Children Who May Need Statements

Circular 1/83 suggests that 'formal procedures should be initiated where there are prima facie grounds to suggest that a child's needs are such as to require provision additional to or otherwise different from the facilities and resources generally available in ordinary schools'. It is acknowledged that this is likely to vary from place to place; the circular indicates that LEAs are expected to afford the protection of a statement to all children with severe and complex learning difficulties in ordinary schools, and all children who may attend any form of special school or unit.

The Act assumes that earlier assessment and intervention is likely to have taken place in school on the lines of Warnock's five stages of assessment, and that parents will have been aware of and, ideally, will be participating in this.

Local authorities vary in their practice, but increasingly they expect schools to provide some sort of record of problems and of attempts to solve them before a school, with the parents' agreement, asks for formal assessment. Individual authorities have in general indicated their policy towards section 5 – teachers should ensure they know of this and can explain it to parents.

Children Who Have Statements

Actually moving from the stage of needing a statement to having one is a long process. In seeking to give parents plenty of opportunity to comment, and in prescribing 'good practice' in statutory form, the Act has produced a cumbersome machinery of letters and assessments that is taking over a year in some areas, perhaps particularly in those where far more children are going through the section 5 procedure that leads to a statement than were assessed under the previous special education (SE) procedures. When children have a statement this incorporates the advice offered by parents themselves, by teachers, by medical officers, by psychologists and by any other professional concerned with that particular child, and summarizes these (if they are compatible!) in a statement of the child's needs and the provision to be made by the LEA to meet these. This must be in an ordinary school provided that account has been taken of the parents' views, and that education in an ordinary school is compatible with:

a   the child receiving the special educational provision required
b   the provision of efficient education for other children in the class or school
c   the efficient use of resources.

This of course is as vague as the concept of special needs itself, and capable of widely different interpretation. It is probably fair to say that most LEAs would like to educate a greater proportion of children with special needs in ordinary schools, but find they cannot do so responsibly without considerable resource implications that are problematic in the current financial climate.

Because of local variations it is difficult to comment in detail.

Perhaps the universal roles of any primary schools who have children with statements are to ensure they have easy liaison with parents, and to ensure that any resources specified in the statement are provided – or any not specified but obviously needed are noted when the school reviews the child's needs on an annual basis.

All Children with Special Needs

If one considers the whole continuum of special needs from birth through the primary age range, from severe to mild, from temporary to permanent, certain patterns emerge. In general, children with major handicaps or gross learning difficulties or developmental delay are detected, largely by health personnel, before they start school. Occasionally a child may arrive in the reception or nursery class who is significantly outside the range of usual children – perhaps incontinent, unable to walk or having no speech. In such situations most LEAs have speedy procedures that offer an assessment place or home teaching or even extra staff to cope for a period. In extreme cases headteachers can of course either refuse to admit the children or exclude them if they are already on register.

Otherwise the primary school is left with a range of 'ordinary' children. Particularly in the early infant classes it is difficult to make clear judgements when children may have had varied pre-school experiences and could be far more able than initial impressions suggest. However, there is no exception in the Act that suggests that schools can ignore children's special needs until they have or have not grown out of them – there is a requirement that all teachers, all schools, will be watching for difficulties, confirming that there is cause for concern and then planning to help. Such a strategy is appropriate as a first stage for all children – whether to meet and overcome special needs quickly and easily, or as the first stage in a longer sequence that may end in a statement of the child's needs or some intermediate provision.

Ethnic Minority Groups

DES Circular 1/83 emphasizes that children should not be taken to have learning difficulties because the language of their home is different from the language of instruction in school. It also suggests that because it is difficult to determine whether such children have special needs every effort must be made to communicate with the child in his or her own language and to make allowance for cultural differences. There has of course been considerable concern expressed at various times about the disproportionate numbers of ethnic minority group children who have been classified as having learning difficulties, or prior to the 1981 Act categorized as educationally subnormal.

Both children with special educational needs and ethnic minority group children have been the subjects of recent reports, concern, and in-service training plans. It is notable how similar many of the concepts used are. The findings of Lord Swann's Committee of Enquiry into the Education of Children from Ethnic Minority Groups (1985) are published as *Education for All. Educational Opportunities for All* is the title of the Fish Report on provision to meet special educational needs (1985). Broadly, those seeking better opportunities for either group seek changes in teacher attitudes, the avoidance of underachievement, a fair deal for a minority group.

Lord Swann in his summary of *Education for All* outlines the factors often suggested for ethnic minority, and particularly Afro-Caribbean, underachievement – a genetic cause, family structure, disadvantage or deprivation, racism in school and society, 'informal' school structure and ethos, LEA failure. He continues by highlighting the 'fallacy of the single factor' – participants tend to hold by a single explanation when a complex one is inevitable; there is also a tendency to generalize – all such children fail, when they do not; a single explanation must be universally applicable, when it is not.

The combination of ethnic minority grouping with possible special needs is one that must be questioned. For all children it may be sensible to seek to identify their problems and then challenge the appropriateness of the special needs label. For children from ethnic minority groups it must be especially relevant to do so, to be quite sure that one is not compounding the sorts of assumptions that have been highlighted by Lord Swann with the identification of special needs. In later sections reference is made to the need for extra care in using some techniques with children from these groups.

The Gifted

The gifted were specifically excluded from the brief of the Warnock Committee and it seems to be assumed that the Act does not cover them. However some voluntary groups have suggested that they may challenge this assumption. Certainly the continuum of need, and the demarcation of curricula, could include the gifted, as an extension. One suspects that many LEAs would see the extra provision of extended curriculum as the concern of the school, without reference to the Act.

The gifted, however, are not separate from the special educational needs population. Some gifted children who are bored can quickly present a problem in the classroom, and most psychologists have met children whose unidentified ability contributed to the problems concerning the teacher. Some have also met the problems of ceiling effect, when able children are put on a programme to work their way to the top group, but have not understood the limitations to a swift upward progress. One unnecessary problem was created when a six-year-old boy was set targets for each table or group so he could move from the lowest to the top where he plainly belonged. His calculations estimated the number of groups in each older class, the numbers of forms in the secondary school, his mean time per group, and a university career beginning at middle junior age. The reality was less appealing!

This book focuses on children with difficulties – we cannot argue in each section that at the same time teachers must plan for the gifted, for racial awareness, for a more integrated curriculum, for the deprived majority who have no identifying label. Of course we recognize that many demands are being made on primary schools while resources, manpower and materials may be limited. Good schools have to invent their own way of integrating all these concerns – while giving the wider range of children with special needs the provision now required by law.

Implications for Primary Schools

There are clear implications for primary schools in the Act. Some may be involved in meeting the specified needs of children with statements. Many are likely to offer educational advice on children who are being statemented. All are going to need to have a special needs policy that ensures that any child with special needs is identified and helped, and a record keeping system to facilitate and help in monitoring this. All are obliged to involve parents if a child has special needs, and to do so in a way that is acceptable, supportive, allows the parents a role that is that of partner in their child's education. The suggestions in this book are intended to help such developments to take place alongside others that schools are pursuing.

CHAPTER 2
The School and Other Agencies

The Range of Support

Local authority schools are unlikely to face the implications of the 1981 Education Act in isolation. The LEA of which they are part will be implementing the Act and have various procedures and policies. It will have an Inspectorate or Advisory Service which offers suggestions, guidance, in-service training; the psychological service is probably offering a different range of advice and training. Visiting or peripatetic teaching services and special school staff may offer other training options. Teachers may be liaising with psychologists or visiting specialist teachers, or education social workers, about individual children who have problems. District health authority staff such as school doctors, child guidance psychiatrists and speech therapists, may also see children in school, and paediatricians and other specialists see them elsewhere. Social workers from the Social Services Department will be involved with some children. There is a formidable range of possibilities although many primary schools will see such support staff infrequently, perhaps less than they would wish. At the other extreme, some special school teachers despair of ever seeing their class as a group since a significant number are withdrawn by support staff at any time.

Variations in LEAs' Policies

The variation in local authority policy and practice in response to a short Act of Parliament is remarkable. Surveys such as those undertaken by the National Association of Principal Educational Psychologists (Pearson, 1985), suggest that even the proportion of children being statemented may range from none to about 5 per cent of the school population. Authorities may see the integration of children with severe learning difficulties or special needs as normal practice so not appropriately subject to section 5; others may accept that a significant percentage need a statement to ensure the continuity of resources. If this sort of variation exists in the formal statutory process, it seems safe to assume that the wider aspects of the Act result in even greater differences.

The two wider developments suggested for LEAs are the priority of in-service training for all teachers, and the establishment of resources of teachers' expertise that schools can draw on. One's data are impressionistic but it seems likely that some authorities have as yet made little attempt to put significant resources into either, some have espoused both, but many have given priority to one or the other rather than both. Many may have intentions to implement schemes still known only to those planning them. It would be worrying if authorities who are training teachers in every school did not see an additional need for specialist support teachers to be available with a range of expertise to advise and help. Conversely, it would be equally unbalanced to assume that a special needs teaching force outside the schools obviated the need for providing information and training for the teachers in schools who have the daily management of considerable numbers of children with difficulties or needs.

It is of course a truism that the Act needs resources that have not accompanied it. Senior administrators in the DES must have heard variants of that statement on innumerable occasions. The *ACE Special Education Handbook* (1983) is only one of many commentaries on the Act that draws unfavourable comparisons with the Education for all Handicapped Children Act (PL 94–142) in the USA and its relatively lavish funding. An alternative view of the situation is that we have had time to adjust to recession management but make heavy weather of it.

Surveys of our national expenditure on beer or continental holidays or of what teenagers spend on records or clothes hardly confirm the major recession hypothesis. There is money for priorities – and whether LEAs see resources and training for special educational needs as a priority is an issue teachers can hope to influence. It is also a decision schools themselves have to face, and it would be naive to expect all to make it a first priority without strong leadership from the authority. Perhaps for primary schools with their history of caring class teachers and a familial ethos it is an easier priority to adopt and to explain to parents than for secondary schools who are often judged by parents on the basis of their results in public examinations.

Different Perceptions of the Act

Not only the interpretation of the Act is variable, but different groups had widely different expectations. Voluntary groups concerned with different 'handicaps' variously saw children who had previously been categorized under the 1944 Act becoming fully integrated, or children whose problems were not a category being recognized and having special provision. Some parents saw it as a charter, a new status, even a weapon to help them fight education authorities – others are more concerned about the waiting involved before a child has a statement and appropriate provision. Professional groups who have little role in the Act seek more – psychologists and medical officers who have a statutory involvement are overwhelmed in many areas of the country.

It is still early to make any firm predictions. What does seem to be emerging is that the statute to ensure good practice is itself subject to good and bad practice. The Act alone is not going to improve things, although in many areas and services it has been a trigger for productive change. For all concerned in it, it is reality, it will not be repealed for many years, it can be used as a stimulus for development and improvement.

Integration

Integration is a process, not a simple situation or product. The Warnock Report describes integration as: 'the central contemporary issue in special education', labelled 'integration' in the UK, 'mainstreaming' in the USA, 'normalization' in Scandanavia and Canada. Integration is an international conviction that as far as humanly possible the handicapped should share the opportunities afforded to the non-handicapped. The Snowdon Working Party on Integrating the Disabled (NFRCD, 1976) described integration: 'Integration for the disabled means a thousand things. It means the absence of segregation. It means social acceptance. It means being able to be treated like everybody else. It means the right to work, to go to cinemas, to enjoy outdoor sport, to have a family life and a social life and a love life, to contribute materially to the community, to have the usual choices of association, movement and activity, to go on holiday to the usual places, to be educated up to university level with one's unhandicapped peers, to travel without fuss on public transport'. The Warnock Report remarks that although this is written of the physically disabled, the passage captures the wider spirit of changing attitudes to the handicapped.

The Warnock Report distinguishes three forms of integration – locational, functional and social. Locational integration is the most tenuous – units or special schools on the same site as ordinary schools. Social integration may coincide with locational integration, but children eat, play, consort together and may share a range of out-of-classroom activities. Functional integration encompasses the others but extends to joint participation in educational programmes. This is seen, whether full time or part time, as the closest form of association, and the one that makes the greatest demands on the ordinary school. When people talk of integration as a 'good thing' they probably refer to functional integration.

Schools and LEAs need to specify what sort of integration is offered, particularly to parents, when children with statements are offered provision. Primary schools, whether they have units or individuals with special needs, need both to decide whether integration is locational or social or functional, and to monitor the effectiveness of this. Individual children may be officially or objectively integrated – but subjectively feel anything but. Effective integration, particularly functional integration, needs a great deal of planning, not least in training peers to offer the right level of help – children rarely ignore someone who needs help, but they may be overprotective if they are not encouraged to offer the minimum effective help.

The Act offers schools or LEAs the opportunity to integrate many children, or the excuses for integrating few or none. Functional integration involves enormous commitment and effort from the teachers concerned and if this is not forthcoming it is better to avoid situations that will not benefit the teacher, the class or the recipient. When functional integration can be offered realistically and enthusiastically there is growing evidence that this is a positive benefit to everyone involved.

New Roles for Parents

Parents have not been universally impressed by their promotion to partnership. Many seem to feel they have always been responsible for their children, and in a role that entails theirs being the major input. However at the other end of the spectrum many parents are still uneasy about crossing the school threshold and feel intimidated by teachers and schools. Some ethnic minority parents have limited English which imposes an additional problem for communication. Primary schools have a wide range of attitudes to parents. Some have home–school liaison teachers and a policy of all teachers making occasional visits to homes, and of welcoming parents at any time. Others have such rejecting devices as signs in the playground indicating that parents should not pass this point, and if parents have a role this is limited to meetings out of school hours where they can elect parent governors and raise money for the school fund. It is difficult to see how the latter sort of arrangements can be compatible with the inclusion of parents as partners when their children have problems.

Indeed it is difficult to see that focusing on problems is a viable form of partnership, unless parents already feel at home in school, welcomed by the head and other staff, able to make easy contact. On that basis early worries can be shared, parents involved in home activities to complement those of school, more serious difficulties gradually accepted. Conversely, a summons out of the blue, the discovery that one's child has difficulties one did not suspect, inevitably starts any 'partnership' off badly, and the chances are it will never become such, rather a polarized antagonism.

What steps schools take to ensure parental access must depend on the area they serve and the attitudes of their teachers. Perhaps every primary school should spend one staff meeting each year imagining what it feels like to be a parent of a child in their school and how communication could be improved and developed. This may still entail a clear demarcation between what teachers do and what parents do, with mutual respect for separate roles, or it could lead to greater parental involvement in the educational process in the sorts of developments outlined in Chapter 9.

Broad Issues Schools Need to Clarify

Primary schools need to have plans and policies for special needs that mesh into their existing curriculum, record keeping systems and other aspects of school policy. How detailed this is will vary, but certain key areas must be included. Broadly these are:

A common policy for identifying children with special needs
Strategies for helping identified children
An individual record keeping system that can include more
    detailed records of such strategies than might normally be
    kept, and which can be open to parents and include records of
    their involvement
A policy of involving parents that is monitored and reviewed
Agreed arrangements with visiting teaching services,
    psychologists and other support staff.

While some LEAs may offer 'instant' policies to schools such documents tend to collect dust in cupboards or filing cabinets. Policies that teachers have discussed and agreed themselves are likely to be pursued. Clearly the head or particular post holders will need to encourage and to monitor the effectiveness of new developments.

CHAPTER 3
A Framework for Special Needs

Planning for Special Needs

The first chapters have taken a broad look at the Act and at aspects concerning schools. This is a relevant context in which any special-needs developments are appropriately placed. However, a school framework, plan or policy for special needs has to tackle these broad issues in a fairly precise way. In some areas the LEAs' comprehensive in-service training of teachers from every school will facilitate planning – in other areas schools may have less help. The best established training scheme is probably the Special Needs Action Programme (SNAP) developed by Ainscow and Muncey (1984) in Coventry, and now published. This is a modular course which is still being extended. Its aims are to encourage headteachers to develop procedures for the identification of special needs, to assist teachers to provide an appropriate curriculum for such pupils, and to coordinate the work of the various special educational services and facilities supporting teachers in ordinary schools.

Authorities or schools buying SNAP can use it flexibly. In Coventry each school has a teacher who has been trained on the total package, and who is the special needs coordinator for that school. Other authorities are using psychologists, teachers and advisers to develop alternative training packages. This is a major commitment – of time to develop and evaluate, and by trainers and teachers and schools if every school participates. Ideally more than one teacher in each school might be trained to ensure continuity when staff move or are promoted to senior posts, and to provide support for each other and a double or treble resource for the school. However, this is even more demanding of resources and time, and may not be practicable.

Whatever training and support is available, schools need to translate their general concerns about children with special needs into a practical plan or policy or framework. A key initial question to decide is the level of planning that will be appropriate. This will be different for a school that has very few pupils with special needs, for one that has a significant number, and for one that is overwhelmed by such children. In each case it is appropriate to ensure that there is a system for identifying children, resources for helping them and a good bridge to parents. For occasional or unusual occurrence the focus would be on accommodating an individual child with reference to the existing curriculum, record keeping system and organization. This would plainly be impractical if most children have special needs – in that case the curriculum, record keeping and organization would need to have a marked overlap with the special needs plans – indeed they might be indistinguishable.

If that sounds like an impractical dream, it may be encouraging to know that it can be achieved – with a lot of commitment from teachers. A Birmingham infants school in a deprived area realized some years ago that major planning was needed if they were to offer appropriate education. Most of the children admitted to the school lacked the skills and experience of ordinary reception class children in such areas as language, self help and socialization. In partnership with their visiting psychologist and subsequently involving a second psychologist, the staff set about creating a new curriculum that would cover the pre-school skills and experience needed and the usual infant curriculum areas. This was in the course of several terms written for the whole school in terms of teaching objectives for each age and area of the curriculum, tried out, modified, and evaluated. This project, GRIP, is described in some detail by Pinney (1984).

This sort of approach would be redundant for many schools, and could only be adopted by a staff who were keen to do so and had support from the head and from relevant advisory staff. However, it is a good example of a school working out what sort of problem it should tackle, and getting on with doing so. Such a systematic problem solving approach is very flexible, and can facilitate planning to some purpose whether the problem is vast, like the school's curriculum, or only one area of one child's learning or behaviour.

Problem Solving Models

Problem solving models are so simple and effective that they can be applied to many areas in education and elsewhere. Howarth (1980) uses a version to illustrate man as a problem solver, Pearson (1980) used a similar model with reference to the assessment of learning difficulties; Pearson and Howarth (1982) use it to characterize professional psychologists.

The simplest basic outline consists of four stages of action and planning:

1   Specifying the problem(s) clearly and recording them
2   Identifying what resources are available to use and noting them
3   Devising a written strategy to make the best use of resources
4   Evaluating how effective the strategy has been and recording this.

This can be a single sequence or one may work through it many times to solve one intractable problem or a series of problems. It is a useful method of considering problems in a way that leads to action rather than complaint or inaction. It can be extended in a range of ways, one being to form a flow diagram which can be a checklist to use. Figure 3.1 shows such a diagram in this case applying the problem solving model to individual child problems, and the teachers' intervention.

This uses the four basic stages above, but extends the first and third into two stages so the diagram shows six stages, and some decision points are shown in double boxes. The first two stages (boxes 1a and 1b) require the teacher to specify the problem – this may start with the result of an identification procedure, to which will be added other observations, perhaps discussion with other adults who know the child and with parents. The problem has to be stated in a way that lends itself to solution, and allows the teacher to check easily if goals are relevant. A problem could relate to an unacceptable set of behaviours, or an area of the curriculum the child has difficulty with, or interactions with particular adults or children that are unsatisfactory, or skills like speech or motor coordination that the child has problems with.

Of course teachers often describe problems in a broader context,

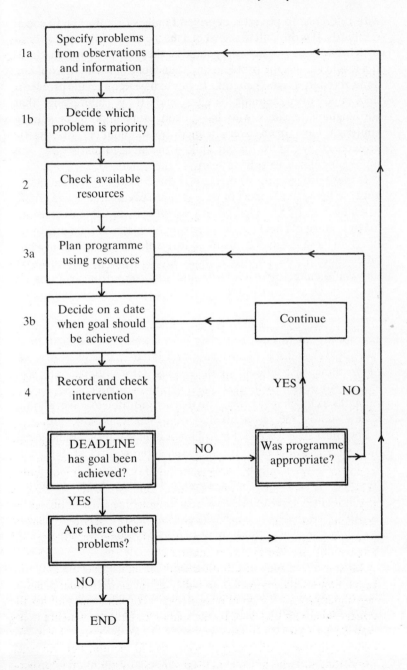

Figure 3.1: Teacher Intervention

with reference to poverty, deprived families or a decline in social standards. It is difficult to see what a teacher could hope to do about such broad issues, or how they could be the basis for helping a child. If a teacher states the problem and then feels that nothing could be done about it, it is too general – better to have ten specific problems than one overwhelming single one! It is interesting that Birmingham teachers who have been using a problem solving approach have been overwhelmed by the number of specific problems they can list for one child – and amazed that solving one often generalizes to solving many of the others.

If there are several problems it is difficult to tackle them all at once, so the second aspect of the problem specification stage (1b) is to decide which to tackle first. It may often be sensible to consider the next stage of checking the available resources at the same time. If a child has a range of problems with particular skills, but also hits other children, the priority is likely to be stopping the behaviour that can damage other children and stop them from learning. If there is no clear priority of that sort, it may be sensible to opt for the easiest resources.

Resources (box 2) in this sense include books, worksheets, appropriate materials. But they also extend far beyond that. Individual class teachers are a major resource – particularly in areas where they are confident of their skills. Other humans are also major resources – visiting teachers, parents, volunteers. So are the strengths a child has to offer. The teacher or problem solver should review and list the resources that are available and relevant.

The third stage (box 3a) is to plan a practical programme using the resources available with a clear goal or target – a clear statement of what the child will be able to do, or will have stopped doing, at the end of the programme if all goes well. Teaching objectives, which are more precise statements of each step in a programme, are described in Chapter 7, a teaching goal or management goal should be on the same lines – observable, unambiguous, understood by the teacher, and by the child as well.

At the same time as specifying the goal, the teacher should make a reasonable estimate of how long will be allowed for reaching it – days, weeks or months (box 3b). It is important to allow enough time for a programme to have a chance to work, but to control this so that an ineffective programme does not drag on.

The final stage involves the teacher and others involved checking regularly that the programme is being implemented and that it appears appropriate, and is recorded carefully. The first double box is the deadline, when the teacher should evaluate whether the goal has been reached. If it has, the teacher should consider whether there are other problems – if not the intervention has been successfully completed; if the child has additional problems a further intervention could be started.

If the goal has not been reached the teacher should consider whether the intervention is appropriate. If it is, but the target time was too short, the programme should be resumed at box 3b; if not, further intervention should be started at box 3a. In general, a teacher should work at least once through the sequence shown in Figure 3.1; after this initial attempt he or she should use their own judgement as to whether further intervention should be designed, or whether advice from colleagues, head, psychologist or adviser would be helpful.

The same model or an adaptation of it can be used to address problems at the school system level – how to involve parents, how to improve the teaching of language, how to provide for a group of children with similar problems, how to integrate a child with a statement. It can be used by individuals or by a group of teachers or by a whole staff. The four basic stages of clarifying the problem – specifying the available resources, planning to use the resources, specifying what should be achieved and monitoring the outcomes – provide a useful record to make what is being done clear to those doing it. It also makes it clear to advisory staff or others who might help so that involving them is easier.

Positive and Negative Approaches

Special education has a history of changing terminology that reflects a wide concern that approaches should be positive rather than negative and should focus on children's assets rather than their deficits. At one level this can become a trivial concern with labels. Many LEAs have a history of changing special school names in the 1950s and 1960s. Changing Gas Street Institute for Imbeciles to Gas Street Special School to The Lilacs, Gas Street, did not stop the local populace calling it the 'daft school'. Changing the label did not significantly affect attitudes. The replacement of the old categories of handicap by the concepts of special needs and learning difficulties could be another example of label change – unless attitudes change as well.

At a less superficial level some teachers, psychologists and others have espoused positive approaches and rejected negative ones in a way that seems naive and potentially unproductive. The important thing is to distinguish between labelling the child and describing his or her behaviour. Labelling of any sort can be offensive and can cause unwarranted concern to parents, so although the implicit message which parents receive is almost inevitably that there is a problem, the approach should be that as far as possible this problem should be looked at in terms of the skills or knowledge the child needs to acquire.

It is a matter of concern if the rejection of deficit models or an insistence on using some words and not others prevents children getting help. Because this is a stance that some individuals take, it seems worth stressing that problem solving can and should be a positive process that entails positive outcomes.

The Range of Special Needs

The consistent interaction throughout a child's school career is with the curriculum, and the greatest number of children have needs relating to learning difficulties. These may be mild, moderate or severe. They may be general or specific to one area. Specific learning difficulties are usually associated with literacy skills – reading, spelling, writing – or numeracy skills. But they can also concern areas that children learn incidentally rather than as an area of the curriculum. First language acquisition is an obvious example – and a complex one since language problems can limit many other areas and have implications for the method as well as the content of teaching.

After learning difficulties, and often interacting with them, emotional and behaviour problems form the largest grouping. Again such problems can be mild or moderate or severe, temporary or longer term. Salient issues for teachers are how disruptive such problems are and whether other children may be hurt or distracted. But it is probably equally important to discover whether they are, like learning difficulties, general or specific, and whether they are reasonable or unreasonable from the child's angle.

Smaller numbers of children need arrangements to access the ordinary curriculum. Access to school buildings, and to appropriate sport and play activities for children with physical disability, is of wide concern and most LEAs have plans to develop this. It is equally important to offer changing facilities for the incontinent in ordinary schools, and access to nursing supervision for children on variable drug schedules. For children with sensory impairment aids for vision and hearing will be needed; so will the technical expertise to maintain, adjust and mend such equipment.

Chapter 5 covers resources, as do the later chapters on specific approaches. It is implicit in the term 'special need' that this is not something within the child, but interactive. Children need help or resources or access – all of which involve interaction with a person or the curriculum or the environment. Schools cannot only plan for each individual child as a problem arises. Some overview of resources and potential for meeting needs is essential. Even if a school has ramps and lifts, has a permanently staffed changing room, uses precision teaching and programmes with parents, has staff who are skilled in solving behaviour problems, resources will only be effective for a limited number of pupils – too many and the resource, whether physical or human, cannot cope. A framework for special needs cannot work without some notion of quantity as well as quality.

CHAPTER 4
Identifying Special Needs

The Range of Identification

If teachers or a school are using the problem solving model outlined in the last chapter, it is apparent that the identification of special needs can be seen within that model in two ways. Identification is the first stage of specifying a problem before moving on to estimate resources, trying to help, checking on the outcomes. It can also be identified as a problem in its own right. If a school or a teacher is focusing on working out plans to ensure that children with special needs are detected, that can be the problem and the problem solving model can then be applied to it.

While it makes sense to see the planning of a procedure to identify special needs in isolation while one is giving it priority, it is not an end in itself. Discovering that 1 per cent, 10 per cent or 50 per cent of a class or school have special needs is utterly pointless unless it is linked to plans for helping them. Chapters 6 and 7 describe two very different aspects of identification. The use of early identification procedures as outlined in Chapter 6 helps to identify only, although it is suggested in the checklist at the end of the chapter that one criterion for selecting such a procedure is its usefulness and relevance to helping. The assessment through teaching model outlined in Chapter 7 is an integrated model that offers a different form of identification which is subjective but leads straight into help for pupils.

These two very different approaches seem incompatible in that they derive from different models, different countries, different priorities. At present, and in the foreseeable future, both have evidence of being effective and efficient, but neither offers a total and comprehensive plan which meets all the concerns a teacher or a school might have. In Chapter 1 the need to relate children to as broad a context as possible and the need to accommodate or meet problems that exist with reference to the class or immediate peer group was highlighted. Of course these overlap in many instances. It is useful to check on a child's place in a broader context – but probably a criterion-referenced approach will be needed to lead to programmes of intervention or help. The two approaches described in detail illustrate the range of approaches available, but they are not the only ones.

Observational Techniques

Some of the LEA training packages and many psychological services are offering a range of checklists to help teachers to structure their observations of children's progress. These work rather like an identification procedure but are informal, and while they assume what skills are appropriate, and in what order, they do not provide any normative comparison. They also resemble the assessment through teaching packages in that they focus entirely on what children can actually do in curriculum areas and may therefore also indicate suitable areas to teach next. Teachers' practice, and consequently their interest in checklists of learning skills, varies. On the problem solving model such checklists would aid teachers in identifying and defining problems at the first stage of the model. Some teachers are extremely adept at doing this without such aids. Others may feel uneasy about a child but find a list of skills helpful in pinpointing difficulties.

Checklists are aids to observation, but teacher observation per se is necessary both to discover problems and to pinpoint them. It is a natural sequence – unstructured observations make one concerned in a general way and one then starts looking more carefully to see exactly what is the cause of concern. For learning difficulties there are plenty of aids, but when children's behaviour is the cause for concern observation is equally vital in specifying the problem. As is outlined in Chapter 8 many teachers and psychologists find the ABC model helpful in specifying and remedying behaviour difficulties. A stands for antecedents, B for behaviour and C for consequences. Teachers who adopt this model of analysing behaviour need to observe all three aspects before they tackle the problem. Even teachers who find this approach too mechanical can gain a lot of information by observing carefully how often the unacceptable behaviour occurs, and in what circumstances.

Good teachers cannot be observers all of the time. However,

there are many parts of lessons or group activity when the teacher who has a framework of useful observations to make can switch from an involved participant role to one of observer. In a very short period of time it is practicable to observe or check what is happening on a number of dimensions. If, for example, time on task is the best predictor of children's academic success (Keogh, 1982) regular observations of on task behaviour would be useful. Checklists or observation schedules can be a great aid in structuring what is observed, whether supplied to or produced by the teacher.

Record Keeping

The level of record keeping is a key factor both in its own right and as an indicator of what other forms of identification techniques would complement the records. Good records of children's levels of achievement of skill acquisition are a general ideal, but they are particularly useful for children with problems, both in identifying the problem and in recording what help has been offered with what result. This is a good factual basis to share with parents or with visiting teaching services, or psychologists or advisers. The level of recording, given the time needed to maintain regular records, is likely to vary, being increasingly detailed with increasing concerns. Using the techniques described in Chapter 7 as applications of the assessment through teaching model generates detailed daily records for areas of concern. Using tests or teacher rating scales produces results for the records but these need to be linked to further data collection or plans for intervention if a difficulty is apparent.

Tests

Many schools use tests of attainment and some attempt to assess general ability by using tests of verbal and non-verbal reasoning. The checklist for early identification procedures at the end of Chapter 6 is broadly applicable to other standardized measures, and certainly the need to ensure that the content is relevant is a primary criterion. It is regrettably true that some teachers seem to have an uncritical belief that any published test is efficient and relevant. Consequently one finds that children who should be reading widely, using a library filing system and book indexes, developing different reading skills for extracting detailed technical information and for light reading for personal amusement are tested on single word recognition tests that demonstrate basic phonic decoding skills. Other teachers use tests that sample reading to some purpose but which also check speed by imposing a time-limit. It seems self evident that the same global scores on such a test can denote very different reading ability. Making no errors but only completing a third of the items suggests that a problem is one of speed. Completing the whole test but only getting one-third of the items right has very different implications. Quoting a reading age or a reading quotient without checking to see why this is low is a waste of the time spent in administering and marking the test. Giving such a test without first seeing what it samples, or what it could highlight, seems equally pointless.

Tests of hypothetical abilities like intelligence or non-verbal reasoning are subject to just the same constraints. Such tests are not magic, and they are culturally biased towards the group for whom they were devised. They sample skills that are incidentally learned – and it makes sense to scrutinize the items and ask whether children have had chance to learn them, and whether they have all had similar chances. Not being able to answer correctly questions that demand answers outside one's experience is neither unintelligent nor unreasonable. It is difficult to see what schools gain, or seek to gain, from such tests.

Probably the main justification offered relates to some notional idea of potential which relies on an assumption that a high score on a measure of general ability entails success in a range of other areas of attainment. While there is a correlation between most tests of any sort of ability over large populations it is erroneous to apply this to individuals. Virtually all standardized tests are adjusted when the norms are calculated so that they provide a measure that is normally distributed. Drawn on a graph this resembles an inverted letter U. Such a graph has the numbers of children on the ordinate or vertical axis, and scores from the very low to the very high on the abscissa or lateral axis. Only low numbers obtain extreme scores, large numbers average ones. Because reading and mathematics and general ability conform to the same pattern – as do height and weight – it is assumed that individuals also do so. This is plainly absurd if one were to consider weight and mathematics. No-one would accept that extremely fat children were brilliant at mathematics and very underweight ones virtually unable to add two and two to make four! While the correlation for tests of ability and attainment is significant, any teacher would expect to find differences if say two test scores were listed in parallel for the class. Interestingly the differences between scores on, for example, mathematics and reading, or verbal reasoning and spelling, can themselves be graphed and they also appear as an inverted letter U or a rough normal distribution curve. In other words, while the largest number of children have similar scores, many have differences each way round and at the extremes some have enormous discrepancies each way. This highlights the fact that the failed potential underachiever syndrome is actually equally balanced by the other side of the graph – the overachieving potential plus children! Pumfrey (1977) extends this argument.

Criterion-Referenced Measurement

Criterion-referenced tests do not measure children's abilities with reference to those of other children, but check whether skills have been mastered. It is an elaborate title for what is commonplace in the classroom – a quick test to see if multiplication or the dates of the British kings or the names of common trees have been taught efficiently. However, that level of testing is often intended to motivate the recipients rather than to monitor the effectiveness of teaching. The more useful applications of criterion-referenced tests are to check that key areas are mastered before a child moves to the next. Like all tests, it is also a check on the curriculum and the teacher. If a small number of children fail it is reasonable to offer additional help; if most children fail it calls the curriculum and/or the teaching into question.

The assessment through teaching model uses criterion-referenced testing as an intrinsic part of its structure. Such tests are short and very well defined – checking that one subskill can be demonstrated with specified accuracy and sometimes at a specified speed. Lack of ambiguity is a desirable characteristic of all tests; commercial tests are not always unambiguous – it may be unclear whether a score reflects speed or accuracy or some interaction of the two. Criterion-referenced tests can avoid ambiguity and should aim to do so. They can form the backbone of an identification plan if teachers or a whole staff take the time to consider the curriculum and select some areas that are seen as core or essential ones where key skills must be mastered. These can be checked by using a range of test items that staff agree children should be able to complete, and checking that children in fact can do so. Such items are best developed by more than one teacher so that any ambiguity or unintended difficulty can be corrected. While it would be possible to devise a criterion-referenced test that only the very able would pass, it is usually used as a technique for checking that the minimum necessary skills have been mastered, and to ensure that individuals who have not achieved mastery are helped to do so.

Implications for Teaching

Any identification techniques must be used for some purpose. One reason for using norm-referenced tests or identification procedures would be to place children with problems in a broader context than the class or the school. Schools may have idiosyncratic reasons for using these techniques, and some may be required by the LEA. However, the identification of special needs must include elements that make it easy and natural for the teacher to begin to meet those needs. On the problem solving model, specifying the problem is only the first stage. It is difficult to imagine that any model could sensibly justify a list of children with special needs being generated as an end product that no-one need ever take any further. Identification must lead to intervention. Therefore it makes sense to plan the practice of identification to be as helpful as possible in doing this.

Two other criteria are also very important. Identification must be fair. It must not for example discriminate against children from ethnic minority groups, and plans that rely significantly on norm-referenced materials would be unsuitable for use with such children. It must also be easy to explain to parents and others. When a school has a special needs policy that includes various identification procedures and routines it may be helpful to tell all parents about these. It is probably easier to cope with a problem if one understands that such problems are common, are expected and are identified routinely by the schools who then always involve parents.

Finally many of the possible avenues – checklists, procedures, assessment through teaching – once recorded and organized, are very popular with children, and both productive and enjoyable for the teacher. Identifying children's needs really can be very satisfying and a very positive experience for all involved.

CHAPTER 5
Resources and Meeting Special Needs

School Organization

This must reflect the school and to prescribe organization in detail would be pointless. It is, however, universally true that moving from some sort of general awareness to a practical policy requires someone to undertake a great deal of hard work. While this could be a head or a specially designated teacher, there are limits on how far teachers – or any other group – accept innovation from outside or above. Even if they accept it, it may be another document that collects dust, whereas procedures and policies that teachers have been actively involved in preparing have more impact for longer. One useful strategy is to involve all staff in agreeing a very broad framework – perhaps to adopt a problem solving model, to give priority to particular concerns, to consider certain approaches in preference to others, and then to allocate more detailed investigation and preparation to individuals or small groups.

The organization for meeting special needs must match the policy for identifying them. If identification is designed to highlight problems without specifying them, the help offered will need to do this as a first stage. If an assessment through teaching approach as outlined in Chapter 7 is used, the identification and provision for children with learning difficulties will be contained in a single framework. Schools with a high proportion of children with special needs will have to devise a more comprehensive approach than those with few. Schools that have children from ethnic minority groups will need to consider the special needs of these groups: for example, the need for communication to be considered as a separate issue, the need to avoid any unfair over-inclusion of such groups as having special needs (e.g. by the use of inappropriate tests).

A school's framework or policy may rely heavily on visiting

teachers or focus on provision by its own staff. It may have a totally shared plan in some detail, or a broad strategy that allows teachers to develop their own approaches. It may be helpful to encourage some teachers to develop particular skills and to become a source of help for others. It may also be useful to pool ideas with other schools who have similar catchment areas and share useful approaches and ideas.

Once a school has a policy or framework or plans to have one it is helpful to check this for its usefulness. Some questions that might be asked initially include:

Is the plan practicable?
Do (enough) teachers have the skills required?
Do (enough) teachers agree and approve the plan?
Are there resource implications?
Can these be met?
Do visiting services have a role?
If so, do they find this an acceptable one?
Has the plan been discussed with advisers and psychologists who
    are likely to work with it in some way?

At a later stage, one could ask

Is the plan cost-effective?
Does it cater for all or most children's special needs?
Does it complement other concerns and developments?
Do teachers find it workable?
Could it be improved?
Is it helping children?
Is it flexible enough to accommodate new developments?
Are parents helped by it?
Are ethnic minority children getting a fair deal?
What changes should be aimed for?
When should it next be reviewed?

Using the problem solving model from Chapter 3 at an organizational or systems level would facilitate policy making or planning.

Resources

Resources are too often characterized as what used to be available and are rapidly dwindling! Of course there have been cutbacks, but resources have not disappeared altogether. Some schools have considerable resources of computers and other advanced technology and may be planning a special needs policy as computer software. Many of the approaches suggested require little in the way of extra educational equipment. They do, however, take time and entail an emphasis on an individual or small group that takes some organization. The key resource is personnel and it may be helpful to consider all the possible resources.

The teacher is the main resource who will be organizing the programme for the child and ensuring that it is carried out and reviewed. This may be in conjunction with the head or a visiting teacher or a range of others. The head has an overall responsibility for ensuring that the school has a plan, but heads who do not teach may choose or be persuaded to participate, either by providing time to work with an individual or small group, or by freeing the teacher to work this way.

Visiting teaching services in some areas may consider a similar role, and may have suitable materials that can be provided for use in programmes of help. As suggested in Chapters 7 and 8, many psychologists have been trained and have access to materials like DATAPAC and PAD. Several of the procedures outlined in later chapters were devised by psychologists and it is worth checking whether the local service has or is developing useful resources. Classroom assistants or nursery nurses can be an enormous aid, not only in the preparation of materials, but as observers, collecting data on a structured basis as outlined in Chapter 8, or in undertaking some of the teaching of individual programmes. So also can parents and children, resources which many schools neglect. Chapter 9 covers a range of joint programmes schools can run using parents as co-teachers of reading, but some parents are also willing to spend time in school on a regular basis if they have a definite job to do. Many teachers – and parents – see difficulties in using parents in the classroom to teach their own children or to work with others when their own child is distracted by a parent's presence. However, it may be worth asking likely candidates if they would consider either using their past experience with younger children, or working with an older group so they will see what their child will be doing while helping children who have problems and adding to skills that will be useful with their own child.

Using children as teachers is plainly unacceptable if the instructor is not going to gain. However, it is possible to structure practice situations so two children take it in turns to be teacher and pupil, or to enable a child to practise a skill to the level where they have mastered it by helping another child on a structured programme. It may also be possible to use secondary school pupils who are following a community programme as a resource. Many Paired Reading Projects, for example, have used older pupils to work with children with reading difficulties and there is much evidence for the effectiveness of peer tutoring in certain circumstances.

There is of course a limit to the number of helpers a classroom can contain or one teacher practically organize and keep supplied with materials. Any new venture should be for a limited time with only one helper; some teachers seem to thrive on helpers and can manage several with great success.

The Content of Intervention

This is as wide as the range of ideas teachers can generate. The examples provided in Chapters 7 to 9 focus on very different sorts of approaches. The assessment through teaching model is a structured approach to learning difficulties; it is still adaptable and available in various forms and packages leaving the teacher considerable flexibility. It derives in part from applied behavioural approaches, but more perhaps from instructional developments in the USA. The suggestions for helping with individual behaviour difficulties (Chapter 8) are similarly structured and overlap in the models they derive from. The techniques of classroom management are rather different, and so are the various models of joint work with parents described in Chapter 9. All have been used successfully by schools and teachers, and while suddenly adopting all of them would plainly be overwhelming, it does not seen sensible, as is emphasized in Chapter 10, to see them as incompatible or in competition with each other. What schools and teachers do to help may well be less important than the existence of a policy and practical ways of implementing it to ensure that children are offered appropriate programmes of some sort, and spend time learning.

However, children who are identified as having special needs are likely to have already failed to learn in the ordinary situation. Offering more of what has already failed is often ineffective.

Structured approaches that allow the teacher to work in small steps to achievement would be redundant for many children but seem to work well for children who have a history of failure. It is also useful to know exactly what such children have learned and to check later that this has been maintained. For many children with learning difficulties there is a considerable gap between just grasping a skill and having learnt it to the level where it is established and likely to be retained. Whereas some very able children are bored by repetitive practice of skills they learn very quickly, children with general or specific learning difficulties may need far more practice to master skills. In Chapter 9 mention is made of the poor record of many remedial programmes which boosted children's reading but had no long-term effect. Learning in the basic subjects is often hierarchical and it is essential to check that children have the skills assumed for a new area before starting on it. While this is particularly vital for children with special needs it can also be useful with a wider group.

When to Statement

Our emphasis for both identification and intervention is on the Warnock 20 per cent, or the large numbers of children who have special needs at some time which can be helped in the ordinary school. However, help will not always be effective and teachers who have tried a range of problem solving approaches, or even one which has had no impact at all, will be concerned to get the appropriate resources for a child. While LEA practice varies, as is mentioned in Chapter 2, most offer support from visiting teaching services or special school resource centres, and all have a psychological service. All have issued guidelines to schools on the particular procedures that are required before section 5 can be initiated, or on the provision available without the formal section 5 assessments and an eventual statement.

Most entail some consultation with specialist teachers and with psychologists. The sort of data collected on an individual problem solving approach is a good basis for such consultation, and for the education advice provided by the school for children who are being considered for a statement. It is also a good basis for communication with parents who should be partners in such provision, and who must be made aware of any intention to provide a statement. Also such an intervention can provide a 'culture fair' or unbiased attempt to help children from ethnic minority backgrounds. A statement is protection for a child – ensuring resources that are not usually available. These might be access to a restructured curriculum, or a small group that helps children with marked difficulties with behaviour. Within the guidelines of the authority, seeking to protect a child with a statement is not an admission of failure but a sensible decision to provide extra resources. Unless a child has a gross problem it is likely that the LEA will expect the school to have already tried to help within its own resources and to base any request for section 5 on that data. However, while providing this, teachers should also be realistic – the section 5 procedure is a lengthy one and should not be started before the teacher, the child and the class have exhausted their goodwill and capacity to offer help and support.

Part II
Specific Approaches

CHAPTER 6
Early Identification Procedures

Background

The early identification of learning difficulties was promoted by the Bullock Report (1975) and by general concern in the seventies that standards of literacy were falling. This was triggered by Start and Wells (1972) reporting on the latest of a series of reading surveys conducted since the Second World War. Although their conclusion was not that reading standards had declined, but that the improvement in reading standards had ceased, many subsequent publications, most notably the Black Paper of Cox and Boyson (1975) criticized schools for falling standards. Subsequent reports, however, like that of Rodgers (1984), for example, have suggested that Start and Wells' comparison data were anyway flawed, and overestimated reading standards in 1961.

Although the impetus for the development of a range of screening procedures, including those focusing on early identification, is now questionable, the practice continues. Surveys of LEA practices show a marked growth in the seventies and suggest that most authorities adopted and continue to use one or more procedure. Lindsay and Wedell (1982) reported 25 per cent of LEAs screening their pupils in 1972, and 47 per cent by 1976. Cornwall and Spicer (1982) and Gipps and Gross (1984) both found just over 80 per cent in the late seventies and early eighties respectively. Probably most schools in the UK are involved in some form of LEA screening. Some authorities developed their own procedures and since these often took years to develop, try out, standardize and finalize, such procedures are still appearing on publishers' lists of new materials.

LEAs have two separate concerns which are sometimes confused. One is to monitor standards by checking on the achievement of certain age bands. This can be achieved by surveying a representative sample of schools, perhaps 10 or 20 per cent. The second is to highlight any children who have problems. For this of course all children must be involved and therefore all schools. A common practice is to use a standardized group reading test for the seven or eight year olds, and to assume that the data obtained will give a general picture of standards, and also identify children with difficulties. In practice this attempt to kill two birds with one stone often misses both!

The amount of data collected is large and its analysis and comparison with earlier years a formidable task. Some LEAs may achieve this, although there is little published evidence of identified trends from such monitoring exercises. Its analysis by the LEA to identify children with difficulties is equally formidable – and it is the schools which need to know about children with learning difficulties rather than the Inspectorate or the LEA Psychological Service. Schools administer the tests and score them, but most see this as a tedious chore for the LEA and have little hope of gaining useful information from it. Some LEAs are well aware that schools send in returns that reflect what the staff believe may be useful. A school that sees the annual test as producing a league table may teach to ensure that most pupils do well. A school that hopes poor results will lead to resources being offered may take care not to teach to the test. There is such variety in the teaching of literacy skills that it is impossible to imagine a quickly administered group test having contents that appropriately sample the range of skills children have been taught in many schools.

While screening or surveying at 7+ is a cumbersome attempt to see if children have age-appropriate skills, the use of checklists or screening procedures at 5+ for the early identification of difficulties focuses mainly on skills that children should have at that age, but which also predict later failure in literacy. Although early identification may be an LEA policy this does not usually emphasize the monitoring of standards, but the provision of information for the teacher and the school. Such information is usually norm-referenced to provide teachers with some broad criteria of normality. To be useful and to justify use by a school or an LEA such procedures must be efficient and cost-effective. Both the authors have developed such procedures and a non-contentious way of offering a critical account of early identification is to use these as examples to illustrate their development and the standards such procedures are subject to.

An Account of Two Procedures

Although the two procedures, the Infant Rating Scale (Lindsay, 1981) and the Bury Infant Check (Pearson and Quinn, 1986) are quite different there are two areas of marked similarity. Both developments were initiated for very similar reasons, and both use very similar approaches to the statistical analysis of their standardization. Both were developed under the auspices of an LEA, Sheffield and Bury respectively, but were designed primarily to help teachers or schools whose approach to identifying children with special needs included a formal procedure. Both were instigated after discussions in the mid-seventies between psychologists and teachers which highlighted complementary concerns. Psychologists were mainly worried about the late referral of many children whose failure had become an established pattern; teachers were interested in a procedure that would help them to help children earlier and offer some broader notion of expected skill level than their particular class or school. They were also interested in participating in the development of procedures which would have a content that they saw as useful and relevant.

Although the concerns were very similar, the actual products that were developed by psychologists and teachers are very different. The IRS was designed to be used with five-year-olds, but also with seven-year-olds. In its final form it consists of 125 items divided between five subscales. All items are five-point scales which the teacher completes from his or her knowledge of the child. The subscales cover language, early learning, behaviour, social integration and general development. The BIC has only one level aimed at second- and third-term infants. In its final form it consists of 60 items, also divided into five areas. One of these areas, learning style, consists of teacher-completed items, and some of the language skills items are also completed by teachers about the child. The other language skill items, and all the items in the other three areas of memory skills, number skills and perceptuo-motor skills involve a response from a child and require the individual administration of items by the teacher or classroom assistant. Teachers can use the teacher-rated items of the BIC as an initial check with all children, and administer the other items to selected children who have low scores.

Both procedures were standardized on over 1000 children drawn from a cross-section of schools. In both cases children from ethnic minority groups were included but there was no attempt to analyse their results separately. The standardization of child-completed items often indicates that some are inappropriate; the BIC at standardization had 100 items, which was subsequently reduced to 60. Both provide indications for teachers of the percentage of children in the standardization who achieved different levels or scores in the subtests and in the total procedure.

Such procedures should be shown to be reliable, and both authors checked this by using test–retest reliability. The IRS and the BIC were both completed twice for the same children with a short gap of two or three weeks in between. In both cases the correlation between scores on the first and second use was greater than .9 indicating that the procedures are reasonably stable and reliable or robust.

Other studies included checks on the interrelationships of the different items and scales. Lindsay (1979a) compared the IRS with a range of individual tests and found that the IRS was the best predictor of later ability. The IRS data were also subject to a stricter analysis (Lindsay, 1979b) which distinguished ten groups of children or ten different patterns of scores. These included children with difficulties in all areas, children with no difficulties, and children who had distinct patterns of difficulties. Because the BIC involves teachers in a test situation which takes about ten minutes for each child, an investigation was made to check that this provided useful information. Four teachers guessed or estimated the patterns of passes and failures on the BIC for each child in their class, and children were then given the BIC items. Three of the four teachers consistently overestimated children's skills, and subsequently reported that the check had highlighted problems they had not been aware of.

While all these statistical and experimental studies add to the useful information about the procedures they do not answer the key question as to whether they identify the children who have problems later. Of course there are limits to the claims the authors would expect to make for a procedure. It would be unreasonable to expect to predict 'O' level results or behaviour problems in the secondary school from a quick sampling of some aspects of a child's functioning in the infant school. However it would seem rather pointless using either procedure if the children who had problems a couple of years later had shown no signs of difficulties earlier. In both cases the authors used standardized tests of reading at seven years to match with the earlier results from the procedure. The BIC study also looked at arithmetic. In all cases the Young Group Tests were used.

A simple comparison of percentages is not very helpful in estimating predictive validity. Even if the procedures and the Young tests both identified 10 per cent of children as having problems there would be no guarantee that the two groups included the same children.

Actually checking this in educational environments is problematic – as soon as teachers are alerted to the possibility that a child has or may have difficulties, they seek to make sure he or she does not! While this is laudable, it means that if the teacher's intervention is successful, many children who are identified as likely to have later difficulties will not do so.

An alternative way of checking predictive validity or efficiency is suggested by Satz and Fletcher (1979). This compares the scores on the identification procedure with the later scores on a test of attainment. Scores on the procedure are divided into those suggesting difficulties and those not. Scores on later tests of reading or number skills are divided into passes and failures. The choice of criteria of difficulty or failing is arbitrary but should relate to those teachers actually use. Children can be grouped into those with difficulties who are identified by the procedure but fail the later test, and those with difficulties who pass the later test. A similar division of children who seem not to have difficulties on the procedure can be made.

HITS & MISSES

BIC or IRS	Later Test	
	Fail	Pass
Difficulties	Hit	Miss
No Difficulties	Miss	Hit

Figure 6.1

From Figure 6.1 it can be seen that these results can be classified as hits and misses – 'hits' when children with difficulties on the procedure subsequently fail a test of attainment, or children with no difficulties pass; 'misses' when children with difficulties pass a later test, or fail a later test when no difficulties were detected by the check.

This latter group is the crucial one to estimate the efficiency of the procedure. Children who have difficulties identified by the check may respond to subsequent teacher intervention, or may have difficulties which persist. Those with no difficulties should continue to succeed on subsequent measures; any who do not, and were not identified as having problems, are a clear measure of the inefficiency of the procedure. In fairness, one may have a very small number of children who have difficulties at a later date because of intervening factors – several changes of school, prolonged absence, illness or other major stresses which disrupt learning, but this should be a very small portion of the total population.

Both the IRS and the BIC show very few children with later problems who were not picked up earlier; in both cases details are provided in the manuals.

Each has had a thorough check that it is an adequate tool, and this procedure has been described in some detail to indicate what teachers might look for in the manuals of other procedures. It would be interesting to undertake further work – perhaps including a comparative study of the two procedures! It would also be possible in an ideal world to change the procedures without many more years of work so that they match better with the current developments in teaching programmes. It is probably impossible to produce a standardized measure with a content that is not dated – if one began again now one's product would be completed in the 1990s and in some aspects out of date.

Criteria for Choosing Identification Procedures

Available procedures mainly fall into two categories: those that require the teacher to make an informed judgement from his or her general observation of the child, and those which consist of specific tasks to be completed by the child either in a group or individually. Some procedures, like the Bury check, use both approaches. While all procedures are designed for use by class teachers, some assume that the teachers can train themselves to administer or follow the procedure, others assume varying amounts of in-service training before the teachers are trained to complete the identification procedure. The time that administering a procedure will take, as well as the time needed to train or practise, are increasingly important considerations as more demands are made on teachers, and basic staffing ratios adhered to more rigidly. Schools will also need to estimate whether they can afford any particular procedure.

A first, practical, issue in selecting a procedure must be whether there is time to do it, and whether the teacher can cope with it readily. Rating scales, like the Sheffield IRS or the Croydon check (Wolfendale and Bryans, 1979) are less time consuming than those which involve children in completing tasks like the Bury check. On the other hand if the teacher's judgement is the measure there is reason to consider whether some in-service training and formal agreement between schools as to ratings would be needed. Otherwise one can imagine that teachers' judgement may reflect their experience.

In general teachers are very aware that they make comparative judgements, not absolute ones, and they wish to have a wider comparison than their own class group. Of course a teacher can and should continue to help a child who is having difficulty with the class work, but it is helpful for the teacher and the child's parents to know if the child is finding a very high standard of work difficult, or is failing to cope by any standard. Primary teachers will be aware of the difficulty of setting a widely accepted standard within a single school with reference to secondary transfer pupils – most schools have been surprised on occasion that a child they saw as having difficulties is seen as relatively able in the larger secondary school group, and vice versa.

Standard scores might be in terms of scores which have been shown generally to indicate that intervention should follow, in terms of percentages of children passing or failing particular items, or the whole procedure may have been developed to sample areas which a child should have mastered. In this case, any failure indicates a real difficulty. The teacher's handbook should indicate how the procedure was tried out to arrive at the standard scores provided. While many teachers, advisers, inspectors, educational psychologists and school doctors have considerable experience in work with young children, and knowledge of child development, one cannot accept that this is adequate to provide a viable check. Authors must produce evidence that procedures work across a representative and reasonably large sample of children. Lindsay (1974) looked at one local authority screening device developed by 'experts' and not tried out with children, and found that some items showed virtually no children as having problems, while others suggested that more than half the children needed help!

Procedures which are practicable, provide some general indication of children with difficulties and show that they have been developed with an appropriate try-out of materials are likely to be suitable for use to aid the teacher to find children who need help. The other vital question is how far the identification procedure actually leads to a programme of intervention – any sort of assessment or identification can only be as effective as the help that follows it. Before examining this question there are various others which can usefully be asked about identification procedures, and which may highlight some strengths and weaknesses of different packages.

It is helpful to know that a procedure does identify adequately the children with difficulties, and that help is therefore being given to the children who need it. It would be very odd, for example, if children were identified by a procedure, but the teacher knew that others in the class had far greater needs.

As indicated above, a 'hits and misses' check on procedures is probably a helpful indicator; a good check should pick up the children who have problems at present and for the next year or two. It seems to us that if it picks up more children than later have difficulties one cannot know whether the check was over-inclusive, or whether subsequent intervention by the teacher worked unless the numbers are enormous. It would seem that some indication of how many children with difficulties one or two years after the procedure were not identified as needing help would be helpful for teachers who would choose the procedure which identified most accurately.

Another query often made by teachers is whether the procedure will tell them anything that a good individual record keeping system does not anyway. A comparison between teacher expectation and a child's actual performance can only apply to procedures which require the child to complete items. Before choosing it may be worth trying a procedure out on one or two children and considering how useful the results are. This could involve not only the subjective opinion of the teacher, but comparing the information with existing records to see if there is already independent evidence of the child's difficulties.

It is also worth looking in the manual to see whether 'reliability' data are provided, either on using the check twice with the same children and showing that widely differing results are not obtained, or getting different teachers to rate the same children and again agreeing. A check which produced widely different results when different teachers used it, or when a teacher re-used it, would not be a very reliable or helpful guide to use.

The link between identification and intervention has already been stressed. Consequently it is particularly important that the identification procedure can lead to intervention. While it needs to meet the constraints above to do this, the most relevant aspect is its content. An inspection of the content of a procedure is a good initial guide to its relevance – examining each item and asking 'What would I do if the child failed that?' If the item is very vague (e.g. language poor for age group), the teacher gets little help in planning intervention. As items show more clearly what a child can or cannot do, the implications for planning become clearer. Of course no procedure will match the curriculum perfectly, or be sufficiently detailed to enable specific teaching targets to be set immediately. A check should indicate problems in broad and relevant areas, and lead to further investigation.

The range of items is equally important. It is all too easy to be impressed with a glossy booklet and to feel that the authors must have more expertise than the teachers. It may be useful to consider what areas are seen by staff as crucial, and then to look for a procedure that covers these. The BIC, for example, includes learning style, but otherwise deliberately omits emotional factors. While the authors suggest that emotional disturbance is not readily or reliably identified for the second term infant group, other procedures do include this, and some teachers may see this as a high priority. On the other hand, BIC includes early number items which are not always available, and this may appeal to other teachers.

It is a truism to say that there is a mystique about tests and assessments, and this extends to published procedures. No procedure is likely to suit every school perfectly; but virtually all have been developed in close cooperation with teachers and are designed to be a useful aid to them. Deciding what to use and indeed whether to use an instrument, should be firmly based on the teacher's evaluation of usefulness. Advice on statistical information can be provided by visiting psychologists, who can be asked to explain it so that any shortcomings are apparent. It would be useful also to find a contact in the authority where the check was developed, and to ask them how helpful they find it.

Before any procedure is adopted it may be helpful for all the teachers involved to take a critical look at it, try using it with one or two children, and then to meet together and rate the procedure.

Some of the things that must be looked at are indicated in this checklist:

A Checklist for Identification Procedures

1   TIME PER CHILD
How long does it take to complete the check for each child?
Does it take a long time to work out the scores?
Are these times practicable? Does that amount of time seem worth using on a check for what will be achieved?

2   PRACTICE/IN-SERVICE
Do teachers have to go on courses?
Do you feel you would need a lot of practice before you could use the procedure easily and accurately?
Is this amount of time practicable?

3   CLEAR INSTRUCTIONS AND SCORING
Do you easily understand how to follow the procedure or are you left guessing or arguing as to what the manual really means?
Is it easy to know whether a child has passed or failed, or what score or rating to allocate?

4   INTERPRETING SCORES
Is it clear what the score or rating means?
Is this what you want and will find helpful?
Are there indications of how that score compares with children of that age – if not did you want to know this?

5   VALIDITY AND RELIABILITY
If the check does indicate what scores children in general get, is this based on a reasonable try-out or standardization of at least 1000 children?
Are there data on how the authors checked that children who have problems are identified, and not too many children who do not?
Are there data on how the authors checked that difficulties one or two years later were picked up?
Do the authors indicate that the procedure is reasonably robust – different teachers get similar results, or using the procedure twice with the same child produces similar results?

6   CONTENT
    Does the content of the procedure reflect what you think
       children should be doing at that age, what you are actually
       teaching them? If not, what use can it be?
    Can you see ways that the results will be *practically* useful?
    Does using the procedure lead you into intervention or help
       directly or at least to an intermediate stage that will do so?

7   OTHER INFORMATION
    Do you know any teachers already using the procedure – and
       what do they think of it? What do the psychologist and
       adviser think of it?

8   DECISIONS
    Can you afford the time and money involved?
    Can you justify this in terms of likely benefits?

Comment

If the responses to this checklist are predominantly positive it may
be worth investing in a procedure. What you will get is only focused
on one part of the problem solving model outlined in Chapter 3 so it
can only be one part of a plan for children with special needs. If it is
not balanced by resources to help such children, identifying them
will be a waste of time. Because of the time procedures take to
develop, some of the content may be irrelevant. But you will get a
separate perspective from a different standpoint to other
observations or measures. You will get some idea of a child's
functioning in relation to a range of peers. Whether teachers only
rank their class internally or whether they use any cut-off points
provided is largely a matter for personal preference. However,
great caution should be exercised to ensure that any norm-
referenced measure is appropriate to the children in question.

CHAPTER 7
The Assessment through Teaching Model

Background

'Assessment through teaching' is a term used for a sequence of criterion- or curriculum-based assessment that links directly into a teaching sequence, further assessment, further teaching to form a cycle of assessment and teaching. Historically this development started in the 1960s when there was an increasing dissatisfaction among psychologists and many teachers with IQ or general ability measures as sources of any useful and practical advice. In that period a great deal of work was done in developing diagnostic tests and corresponding teaching programmes. The idea was to measure the perceptuo-motor and psycholinguistic processes which were thought to underlie the acquisition of academic skills and, on the basis of this information, prescribe individualized teaching programmes. Such programmes were designed to be matched to specific profiles of abilities and disabilities.

This ability training approach depended upon demonstrating that programmes benefit pupils differentially according to their diagnosis. In the literature this is called *aptitude-treatment-interaction* (e.g. Gardner, 1977). The aptitude is the diagnosis, the treatment is the teaching programme – the interaction is assumed to justify the other two.

Various studies summarized in Kneedler and Tarver (1977) demonstrated the elusiveness of aptitude-treatment-interactions. A teaching programme developed specifically for a child's particular diagnosis was no more effective with him or her than a teaching programme derived from any other basis. Such findings seem to have been noted, and diagnostic tests of the kind investigated in these studies are no longer used by most psychologists.

Norm-referenced tests of attainment in basic subjects are more frequently used. Much as the IRS and BIC enable teachers to relate children to a wider group and assess their problems in this context, so population related measures offer a general comparison. This is emphasized in Chapter 4 as vital if one is justifying a change of placement or a move from a normal mainstream curriculum to a restricted special one. It is also useful when identifying problems, and certainly parents almost invariably want to know where their child fits with the peer group, not only that a particular teacher finds him or her difficult in some respect.

However, none of these measures leads to a detailed analysis of the child's performance, for example in reading, nor to a teaching programme. Increasingly psychologists sought methods that would lead to practical suggestions, particularly for children with persistent and resistant problems. Work in America deriving from curriculum analysis and behavioural approaches seemed the most likely to be appropriate and underpins the work described below. This is very structured and no-one has ever suggested that all teaching should be so structured, nor that this method is suitable for all or even most children. It is effective, particularly with children who have not learned incidentally or through 'discovery' learning or from ordinary lessons, and whose continuing failure becomes a cycle from which they are unlikely to escape unaided.

For this group of children who fail to learn the basis of reading, spelling, writing or number, a very detailed assessment is needed that leads directly to a teaching programme which is what 'assessment through teaching' offers. This account of the approach is a modified version of that given by Pearson and Tweddle (1984).

The Model

Precise information concerning what a pupil can and cannot do in important skill areas is indispensable for two different, but equally important, reasons. First, a teacher who does not know what the child already knows has little basis for deciding what needs to be taught. For example, in reading, the teacher may need to know which letter sounds are known and not known, whether the pupil can blend phonically regular consonant–vowel–consonant words, which words in a new reading book are not familiar to the pupil. Such detailed information will directly influence what is taught and how. To be unaware of the pupil's existing skill levels in this amount of detail may lead to work at an inappropriate level being presented to a pupil who has already a history of failure.

Criterion-referenced information provides a baseline against which later pupil progress can be measured. It is much more useful in this context to the teacher to be able to record that clearly defined skills have been achieved than it is to know that a reading age has increased from 6.1 to 6.5 years.

A number of practical issues emerge from attaching importance to criterion-referenced assessment. First, data of this kind are out of date as soon as the pupil's skill level changes. Hence, a record of criterion-referenced information is needed to use as the next baseline and as a basis for planning as soon as learning has occurred. Therefore, criterion-referenced assessment has to be a continuous process and not a 'one-off' event. It follows that such a process can be undertaken only by the class teacher, the person who is in regular contact with the pupil, and not the psychologist or other visiting service members.

Secondly, published criterion-referenced tests are useful only in so far as the skills covered by such tests correlate with the skills and knowledge which the teacher intends to teach, i.e. the curriculum. Unfortunately, such a match is rare and, consequently, criterion-referenced tests are required which measure pupils' progress on the school's own curriculum. The curriculum must become the test and vice versa.

This is a redefinition of assessment. By focusing on criterion-referenced measures, as opposed to child-centred individual differences, assessment becomes a continuous process which occurs in the classroom and involves the class teacher observing and recording a pupil's response to teaching over time. Assessment, curriculum and record keeping have become inextricably interrelated, a single integrated process. This has been called 'Assessment Through Teaching' and is diagrammatically illustrated in Figure 7.1.

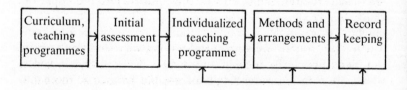

Figure 7.1: Assessment Through Teaching (adapted from Delecco and Crawford, 1974)

Initially the curriculum is used to find out what the pupil can and cannot do. These data are used to decide what needs to be taught and in which order. Thereafter decisions can be made regarding the teaching methods and resources to be employed, and finally detailed records kept of progress made. The feedback loops indicate that the pupil records may lead to changes in methods or the teaching programme itself.

Teaching Objectives

Behavioural objectives, sometimes called 'performance' or 'instructional' or teaching objectives, were defined by Mager (1972). They are descriptions of learning outcomes or, as Gronlund (1970) put it, the 'end products of learning'. They describe what the pupil should be able to do *after* learning has occurred. This represents a major departure from practice in most UK schools. Instead of stating teaching intentions in fairly general terms, behavioural objectives require precise descriptions of the pupil behaviour which will demonstrate to the teacher that a skill has been acquired.

As Pearson and Tweddle (*op. cit.*) state:

Behavioural objectives must contain three important components:
   a   a verb which describes an observable pupil behaviour
   b   a description of the conditions under which the behaviour is to be performed
   c   a description of the standard or *criterion of performance* required of the pupil.

In practice, the conditions described usually contain details of the materials required and the instructions provided to the pupil. For example:

Pupil writes the answer to fifteen single-digit addition sums to totals of ten or less (in the form 4 + 3 =) when asked to complete the sums as carefully as possible, making no more than one error.

Many psychologists and teachers have used a four-column format for writing objectives. This has the advantage of being able to include detailed information in a clear and easily retrieved form. For example:

Material	Instructions	Pupil's Behaviour	Performance
Sheet of 15 single-digit addition sums, e.g. 4 + 3 =	'Do these sums as carefully as you can'	*ADDS SINGLE DIGITS TO TOTALS OF 10 OR LESS*	14/15

Figure 7.2: The Four-Column Format for Presenting Behavioural Objectives

A teaching programme obviously would contain a number of such objectives. An efficient and accurate record keeping system can be developed simply by adding a number of columns to the right side of the objectives (as in Figure 7.3). The first column is used to record the pupil's performance during an initial or 'placement' assessment and the remaining three columns are dated when work is commenced on the objective, when it is achieved and when it is checked.

Initial Assessment	DATE		
	Started	Achieved	Checked
4.10.85			
✓ X	5.10.85	17.10.85	14.11.85
7 8			

Figure 7.3: Additional Columns for Recording Behavioural Objectives

Much of this work was initiated in special schools, and Pearson and Tweddle (*op. cit.*) outline these developments. In the ordinary schools work has undoubtedly been limited by time constraints – both of psychologists and of teachers. The work that has gone on can be divided broadly into two different applications of the same model. One involves teachers in some general training so that they can then write their own programmes; the other offers a bank of assessment through teaching programmes that teachers can be trained to use rather than design themselves.

Applications of the Model

The assessment through teaching model is probably best known in the UK through the training in precision teaching that several authority psychological services offer (e.g. Williams *et al.*, 1980).

Precision teaching (PT) is a misleading title since it suggests a specific teaching package. It is rather an application of the assessment through teaching model as a systematic analysis of any teaching style or method or content. White and Haring (1980) define ten steps:

1 goal setting
2 objective setting and sequencing
3 preparation of assessment devices
4 conducting initial assessment
5 analysing the results of assessment
6 developing a plan
7 implementing the plan
8 collecting progress information
9 charting progress
10 amending the plan as needed.

Formentin and Csapo (1980) have written a guide to precision teaching which is a self instruction manual for teachers. It is a long and detailed book – perhaps excessively so – but PT is or can be technically very sophisticated. Opposite their introduction a cartoon is captioned: 'After the initial shock precision teaching becomes fun'! PT has certain advantages – it is flexible in application, there is a range of record charts and plan charts available, and in some areas support from teacher groups.

PT does not offer any guide to lesson content, whereas some

American developments comprise sequences of scripted lessons. The major assessment through teaching development was initiated, as part of the Headstart programme, at the University of Oregon. Englemann and his co-workers have provided enormous detail about their principles of instruction and vast empirical evidence (Englemann and Carnine, 1982; Carnine and Gilbert, 1979) to support their approach, direct instruction. Their teaching materials are marketed as DISTAR and have been tried out in many schools in the UK. Despite some encouraging data (Maggs *et al.*, 1981) DISTAR is not popular with British teachers. The language of instruction is very American, and the nature of the programmes which consist of scripted lessons in an invariant sequence with scripted homework may mean that teacher preparation is non-existent. It also means that flexibility and modifications are equally non-existent. However some teachers have achieved remarkable results and enjoy this approach.

A British 'compromise' between PT and DISTAR is DATAPAC. This is the most ambitious British development of resource materials for an assessment through teaching approach. DATAPAC is Daily Teaching and Assessment – Primary Age Children (Ackerman *et al.*, 1983). It was developed at the University of Birmingham by a group of educational psychologists to offer teachers programmes in reading, spelling, handwriting and mathematics. Each programme can be used at three levels: a sequence of objectives where the teacher has total control of the lesson; objectives with suggested teaching steps to achieve them: or scripted lessons. Psychologists in many LEAs have attended DATAPAC training courses and have the master files. When a teacher and a psychologist implement a programme for a child with learning difficulties one resource is the appropriate section of DATAPAC which the psychologist can photocopy and provide. In some areas psychologists are now trying out training teachers in DATAPAC so it can become a school resource. 1981 Act in-service training developments like SNAP (*op. cit.*) are also using assessment through teaching models for some parts of the courses, on the same lines as DATAPAC.

Comment

Assessment through teaching is an efficient resource to use with children who have learning difficulties. It comes in a range of approaches from precision teaching which offers teachers a framework for their own programmes through to the DISTAR products which are totally scripted lessons. It is possible to read about these techniques, try them out and train oneself. However, that is a difficult route, and most teachers either attend courses organized by their psychological service, or learn to use PT or DATAPAC by working in partnership with a visiting teacher. Like all other resources that focus on individuals or small groups on a regular basis it is practical if the demand if relatively low. There are many enthusiastic practitioners, and evidence that they achieve good results. However, there are not enough data to suggest that one approach is better than others; teachers should use what they can access and what they find personally useful.

There are issues still to be clarified if research could be funded. There is reasonable knowledge gained from America of what to teach and how to set objectives and measure results. There is little known about the effects of sequence or order on the effectiveness of programmes, and little as to which are the more effective methods of teaching using this model. Levels of fluency in British developments are based on American work (e.g. White and Haring, 1980) and may not be the best for UK children. It would also be helpful to have information about effectiveness with ethnic minority groups although there seems to be no intrinsic cultural bias to the model, and the Headstart programme in America (in which DISTAR was the most effective approach) certainly included a high proportion of black children.

It is an approach which can be seen as closely analogous to the problem solving models outlined in Chapter 3 at a level of greater specificity and detail. Unlike the other approaches to identifying and helping children with special educational needs which can be seen as appropriate to one stage in a problem solving model, assessment through teaching combines all the stages to provide a complete provision for children whose problems are serious enough to justify the time needed.

CHAPTER 8
Managing Behaviour

Background

The identification of behaviour problems has not attracted the interest that has been invested in identifying learning difficulties. For many sorts of behaviour it can probably be assumed that teachers simply could not miss them! Moreover while children with learning difficulties of any significance are universally recognized as having special needs, children whose behaviour is a problem are variously seen as naughty, disturbed, badly brought up, a nuisance. Nearly all these terms are child labels that assume within the child problems which are not interactive, that disown the problem rather than seeing it as one that can be tackled. It is probably fair to say that more statements are made that assume the child is predominantly responsible for behaviour difficulties than for learning problems. If a school's special needs programme is to include behavioural problems, and most would appropriately do so, it may be worth spending a little time first exploring attitudes and trying to find a common framework. This might be in the context of deciding between, or for a mixture of, the two main approaches to problem behaviour.

These have a range of labels but can be broadly grouped into classroom control or management strategies for teachers, and suggestions for teacher intervention with one or more individual children. Since control strategies aim to reduce or prevent problems, but do not eradicate them entirely, it may be most effective to adopt a mixture. Both are applicable to primary schools or children although both are more often the subject of study or practice in the secondary school.

Classroom Management

One of the earlier studies in this area (Kounin, 1970) is still very influential and despite its American background offers many insights and practical suggestions to teachers. His studies looked at teacher–pupil interactions at primary and secondary levels as well as in colleges. Kounin's concern was the practical issue of how teachers should handle children who misbehave. Since teachers are usually operating in a classroom with a large group of children he emphasized the effects on other pupils as well as on the particular child who is misbehaving – what he terms the ripple effect. In a kindergarten in Detroit, Kounin's researchers carefully observed the effects of teachers telling children to stop doing inappropriate things – Kounin's term for such instructions is 'desists'. These studies, like those with older groups, demonstrated that desists have a clear ripple effect – other children's behaviour also changes.

A study of desists led to their being classified along three dimensions: clarity, firmness and roughness. Clarity refers to the information contained in a desist – whether it is clear who is being spoken to, what is to be stopped, what the child should be doing, perhaps suggestions as to what to do instead or how to stop what is objected to or some reference to standards or reasons. A teacher simply saying 'stop that' would not be rated highly on clarity; saying 'James, put the car in the garage and get your work book like the others' would be. Clear desists are, as one would expect, more effective, and they also have a greater effect on other children whether they are also doing something inappropriate or getting on with their work.

Firmness is described as: 'the degree to which a teacher packs an 'I mean it' and a 'right now' quality into the instruction'. This might be shown by following it up rather than seeming to forget it, by continuing to watch the child or walking towards them or speaking emphatically. A firm desist also has some ripple effect but only on children who are misbehaving or watching the child who is. Although this was a positive effect it was less marked than the effect of clarity.

Roughness refers to a teacher's expression of exasperation or anger, by using angry looks or tone of voice, by using threats or physical punishment (although no physical punishment was observed in the kindergarten class). Rough desists emerged as not only less effective than clear or firm ones, they also produced some disruptive reaction. Kounin demonstrates that even a simple and common instruction can be varied to be effective or used in a way that is less so or can even be counterproductive. Once teachers are aware of such findings, they do not need Kounin, or perhaps David Hargreaves (Hargreaves *et al.*, 1975) as a British interactionist to sit in their classrooms. It is quite easy to try different forms of instruction and note how effective or otherwise they are and adopt the best.

Kounin also examined in some detail the interactions between teachers and pupils that occur when teachers initiate or change classroom activities. His terminology is an entertaining and memorable guide to some of the commoner confusions that can be avoided to good effect. These include thrusting, dangling, flip-flopping, overdwelling and being stimulus bound. Brave teachers can have considerable enjoyment and insight from pairing with a colleague and checking each other for such habits. Thrusting is when a teacher breaks in – or thrusts him- or herself – on a group or individual working, without any prior check that this is appropriate timing. It also includes other occasions when no account is taken of signals – perhaps moving without warning to a new phase of a lesson when children are still wanting to contribute to the present one. Dangling is starting something, leaving it dangling in mid-air while the teacher does something different, and then returning to it. This is quite usual – an example would be remembering that children must take letters home or bring their money for an outing and reminding them in the middle of explaining what they must do in the next stage of the lesson. Some dangles can be so lengthy that they take over and become the lesson!

Thrusts and dangles can occur when the teacher is moving from one activity to another, but also in the middle of a lesson or activity. Flip-flopping is a characteristic of untidy and potentially confusing lesson changes when the teacher alternates between the two. A typical sequence might be: that's the end of spelling – get your arithmetic folders – did anybody spell 'charity' right? – I hope everyone has a ruler – how many children got ten right? etc. Overdwelling is literally that, making a long fuss about a minor mishap, making heavy weather of an activity by extending it too long – for example, telling each child when they can leave the classroom for lunch instead of organizing by groups. Being stimulus bound is to be distracted by any stimulus – a lecture on litter triggered by a piece of paper on the floor, or a long reply to a question that does not relate to the lesson.

Robertson (1981) writing of *Effective Classroom Control* does not use Kounin's terminology but makes similar points. He also emphasizes teachers' non-verbal communication skills as a way of conveying authority or enthusiasm that is not always attuned to the verbal message but is often understood by children. His checklist for successful teaching skills is a very useful guide which covers lesson planning, good preparation and the match between activity and group. He also suggests limiting reprimands and using gestures and other strategies to keep children alert.

Classroom management is not specifically aimed at children with special needs. Indeed, like a range of the techniques mentioned, it could be seen as good teaching practice or appear on courses for teachers which emphasize gifted children or working with ethnic minority group children. It is currently an area of interest for secondary schools, partly because the problems of teaching many different groups each week are more apparent than those of class teachers, and also because the abolition of corporal punishment in some LEAs highlights the need for effective control and teaching. The DATAPAC materials developed by a group of educational psychologists seconded to work together for a term are mentioned in Chapter 7; a similar one-term course at Birmingham University produced PAD or Preventive Approaches to Disruption. This covers seven areas, describing pupil behaviour, non-verbal communication, aspects of lesson organization, pupil management, a teaching skills checklist and the observation and analysis of individual pupils' behaviour. PAD materials have been widely distributed, psychologists from many LEAs having attended courses, and being trained to explain the materials to schools and to work in partnership with them on a single area or a range of areas to match the schools' needs. Although PAD is intended for secondary schools aspects could be used in primary schools. The materials are currently being re-written as a resource book for schools.

Individual Pupils

Much of the current work which focuses on helping individual pupils to behave in a more acceptable way which will facilitate their learning and that of the rest of the class derives from ABA. ABA stands for Applied Behavioural Analysis and is a psychological approach derived from Radical Behaviourism or behaviourist psychology. This approach makes certain assumptions; proponents vary between those who appear to see this as the only viable approach which puts some teachers off, and those who see it as one useful approach which seems more realistic. Wheldall and Merrett (1984) are rather prone to talk of 'behavioural teachers' but provide a clear and readable account. They outline the key assumptions as including the teachers' focus on what is observable when describing or trying to change behaviour. This is similar to the assumptions of assessment through teaching described in Chapter 7. It really is very hard to be sure that a child's attitude has changed, but comparatively easy to check that they can read more words or stay in their seat without annoying other children for a longer time. It is also easier to explain the problem and any subsequent success in tackling it to parents if one is not arguing about whether a child does or does not have an interest or attitude, but what the observable problem is and what would be better. Another assumption is that behaviour is learned and new behaviour can therefore also be learned. It may be tempting to blame heredity or home but that does not lead to much change. There is plenty of evidence that children can learn new and less deviant behaviours, just as they learn to read or do sums which are also new behaviours.

ABA also asserts that children's learning is related to a law of effect. They learn behaviours or skills that are satisfying or earn praise or approval – and tend not to learn those that do not. Its proponents usually break behaviour down into three components, sometimes labelled the teachers' ABC. These components are the antecedents (A) or contexts in which behaviour occurs, the behaviour (B) itself, and its consequences (C) or what happens to and for the child.

It is obvious that behaviours do relate to contexts. Some of the more annoying classroom misdemeanours would be quite reasonable in the playground or at home. Sometimes teachers accept behaviour because there is a context for it – for example, not working or crying will be tolerated if a child has been bereaved. At a broad level teachers must look for such causes of changes in behaviour and show sympathy and tolerance as appropriate. Assuming that such antecedents are not apparent it is useful to consider the context in which the problem behaviours occur. It is a basic human characteristic to generalize, and children, like adults, are often labelled as always having tantrums or being a nuisance when in reality this is only in certain contexts. It is useful to observe and to realize that it is only in maths or only with the dinner lady that a problem occurs. It is also a good idea to have a baseline measure. If a child's behaviour is a real cause for concern a record of where and how often it occurs is the first bit of data collection. On the problem solving model this would be part of clarifying the problem, but also useful at the later stage of evaluating the effectiveness of intervention. It is also useful to note any obvious consequences – it is sometimes readily apparent on observation that the 'deviant' pupil actually gets a better reaction from peers or the teacher for unacceptable behaviour than for 'good' behaviour.

Teaching new behaviours or a behaviour change approach is a quick way to try to solve a problem, and therefore a useful initial approach. Westmacott and Cameron (1981) in an optimistic book entitled *Behaviour Can Change* provide helpful anecdotes as well as cartoons in a very readable account of this approach, and one that offers a rather liberal interpretation of ABA.

Changing Behaviour

This fits well, as indicated above, with the problem solving model outlined in Chapter 3. Having spotted the problem, the first stage is to clarify and define it. This might involve the teacher in listing the behaviours that are unacceptable and keeping a record of their occurrence for a week on the lines of Figure 8.1.

		late	talking	out of seat	tantrum
Monday	am pm				
Tuesday	am pm				
Wednesday	am pm				
Thursday	am pm				
Friday	am pm				

Figure 8.1: Record of Unacceptable Behaviour

The teacher can either rely on having a chart handy and noting each misdemeanour, or can opt to do spot checks at set intervals. A popular suggestion is the use of a kitchen timer set to ping at suitable intervals. Many teachers indicate that telling a child that one is using the timer for the purpose solves the problem before one has defined it! If a week's observation using Figure 8.1, or a version of it, shows that the child was only once late, talked on four occasions inappropriately, had no temper tantrums, but was out of the seat when they should have been in it on 11 occasions the first problem to tackle is the latter one. Such problems are often interrelated and in tackling one others can also be reduced.

If the record has been the teacher's first attempt it may be easiest to attempt a simple count, and then spend a further couple of days watching to see what the antecedents and consequences are and whether these help to specify and clarify the problems. With a little experience teachers can often note these at the same time as counting frequency. Assuming that no lack of basic equipment or learning difficulty or obvious pay off is detected the teacher has a good description of the problem which can be shared with the parents, discussed with colleagues, and a suitable programme to teach preferable alternative behaviours set up.

While some suggestions involve elaborate rewards, this is not easy to arrange in a classroom, and tends to be seen by pupils and teachers as unfair – other children who already behave acceptably do not get sweets or lavish praise. Children vary, but many respond eagerly to reasonable praise – that today is better than yesterday, that the teacher is pleased with progress. If a more tangible reward is needed it might be practical to involve the head, or to have a system where a home–school notebook is used and the parent provides a moderate reward when the report from school is positive.

In setting up a programme the child needs to understand clearly what will be a success, and the teacher to have a clear way of monitoring this. This could be the negative one if a reduction in, for example, time out of seat, or the positive one if increasing time in seat and on task. It can be helpful to involve children in their own monitoring, and the ubiquitous kitchen timer can be very effective, perhaps with the child setting it for specified periods and getting a smile as recognition for achievement when this pings. Such an arrangement is flexible so that short periods can be gradually extended to the eventual removal of the timer and occasional praise for staying in seat for the expected period. The key elements are clear objectives, a written record, and consistency. Trying various approaches that the child does not understand for short periods can be counter-productive and confusing.

Comment

Using a practical problem solving approach to learning new behaviours is often successful. It is perhaps unfortunate that some accounts of such work emphasize behaviourist texts and leave teachers feeling that it could be a cold and inhumane approach. Children can be and usually should be partners in what is planned and their parents should agree and can be useful allies. Following the problem solving sequence outlined in Chapter 3 teachers can decide whether they are near to success or whether advice from a visiting teacher or psychologist would be helpful. Of course there are a small number of children who need far more help in changing their behaviour than can reasonably be offered in the ordinary classroom and the problem solving sequence is a part of the data collection that would be needed if a move or a statement were to be considered.

As with all approaches, using behaviour change techniques with children from ethnic minority groups should be planned with particular care to ensure that parents understand what is happening and offer constructive support. It is also helpful to check that cultural differences are not a factor in the problem.

CHAPTER 9
Parental Involvement

Background

The part parents should play in their children's education has been a source of debate for a long time. Well before the Warnock Report was published teachers were divided as to whether parents make good teachers or bad ones, whether they have the right skills or whether only teachers can teach effectively. Of course a lot of teachers are themselves parents and take a keen interest in their own children's learning. A lot of other parents do so too, particularly at the infant and junior or first school stages. Some schools have welcomed this, others have not. Some have developed a wide range of informal ways of seeing parents regularly, others only do so by appointment or at formal meetings or when the parent–teacher association is raising funds for the school.

The 1981 Act does not insist that all parents must be partners in their children's education – but it does require teachers to inform and involve parents if their child has any problems or special needs. Any system which excludes most parents but summons any whose children are having problems could be negative and counter-productive. It seems likely that a system that includes all parents and allows successes to be shared as well as difficulties would be more acceptable. It is very hard to run a double system without it creating problems of its own. If some parents must be included as partners, it is worth considering including all.

In recent years there has been a variety of projects at primary level where parents are involved as partners in aspects of their children's education. The major focus has been on the teaching of reading. These projects can be divided into three main groupings. First there are Parent Involvement schemes. Next there are those schemes that use Paired Reading. A third set has grown out of the last two, either using more complex teaching methods, or combinations of methods.

Reading Projects

The teaching of reading is of course regarded as a central part of the work of the teacher in the primary school. Despite anecdotal evidence, and some derived from the biographies of famous people, which pointed to the fact that at least some children began to read before ever starting school, many teachers have been at best lukewarm and at worst hostile to the idea that teaching reading was a task for anyone other than a trained teacher. This position was adopted not only on the grounds of restrictive practice, but based on a belief that reading is a highly complex skill, that its acquisition is central to a child's educational development, and requires expert guidance.

Several lines of investigation have questioned this assumption. The Plowden Report (Central Advisory Council for Education, 1967) suggested that parents' interest in their children's education was the most significant factor in the level of children's academic achievement. Studies by Douglas (1964) and Davie *et al.* (1972) showed that factors such as the numbers of books in the house and the parents' newspaper reading habits were associated with educational success.

Against this background a study by Hewison and Tizard (1980) produced some fascinating results. They investigated 267 working-class children aged seven to eight years from a council estate in Dagenham. They found that reading achievement at this age was strongly related to whether or not the mother regularly heard her child read, and that the amount of 'coaching', as they termed it, showed a significant positive association with a child's reading test score. Their study provided direct evidence to suggest that parental (maternal) involvement in hearing their child read could help to develop reading at this crucial age when the foundations of reading are developing rapidly.

Subsequently, Tizard *et al.* (1982) devised a project in six multiracial inner-city schools in Haringey which lasted two years, over the top infant and first year junior age range. In a carefully designed study, they examined the progress of children under one of three conditions: regular reading at home using books sent by the class teacher, additional help provided in school by an extra teacher, or no additional help at home or school. Two classes were involved in reading at home, and two classes received the extra teacher help. These four classes were from four different schools; the classes in the remaining two schools, and parallel classes in the other schools provided control groups. The main finding of this study was that the children receiving extra help at home made highly significant progress in reading compared with the control groups, but that no comparable improvement was made by the children who received extra help at school.

The study also highlighted parents' willingness to be involved in a scheme where they listen to their children reading books provided by school on a regular basis. A comparable scheme to the Haringey project was developed in Rochdale at the Belfield Community School. This has been described in a publication by the school itself (see Jackson and Hannon, 1981) and in a chapter in a recent book (Hannon *et al.*, 1985).

At Belfield the teachers initiated a home reading programme and attempted to evaluate its success. Unlike the Haringey research they did not make use of control or comparison groups, but measured success in terms of the performance of the children themselves, and the attitudes and behaviour of their teachers and parents. Their results show that the project led to a substantial increase in the amount of reading at home. About 90 per cent of the project children were reported by their parents to read 'almost daily' to someone at home, whereas only about one-third of the children had read this frequently prior to the project.

A comparison over time shows that children's reading at home reduced over a period of about three years, the drop was not dramatic, and on average children read to someone at home three to four times a week.

These results, and the original booklet by Jackson and Hannon provide evidence that the scheme was highly successful in terms of take-up, and that it was popular with parents and other adults who heard the children read at home (e.g. grandparents). No results have so far been published to enable an evaluation to be made of the possible effect of this project on reading development. On the other hand, the project has influenced several other interesting studies in Sheffield and many other areas.

One study was conducted at Fox Hill First School on a council estate in Sheffield (Weinberger, 1983). This was a school-based project where parents were encouraged to come to workshops run in the school. Children read to their parents, who also had the opportunities for discussion with teachers, and to make games and worksheets. Parents were visited at home to encourage them to join in and to provide materials to any families who could not attend. A booklet provided a description of how the workshops were set up and developed (Smith and Marsh, n.d.). As with the Belfield study, there was evidence that this method of involvement was very popular with parents, and with teachers. Evidence of improvement in the children's reading is limited to judgements by teachers who considered that a third of the children had progressed better than expected.

A study reported by Sigston *et al.* (1984) in a junior school in Barking and Dagenham combines the work of parents and teachers in hearing the children read. Both agreed to hear the child read a specified number of times per week. The length of each session at home was also agreed – 'three egg timers'. In addition the teachers agreed to check the record forms completed by the parents and follow up phonic worksheets provided by the headteacher.

The parents heard their children read far more often than they had before this project began, and reported very favourable opinions of it. Thirty-one of the thirty-three children showed higher reading ages at the end of the project. The rate of reading improvement, compared with that achieved since school entry, almost trebled. Interestingly, there was some evidence that greater gains were made by the children whose initial reading age was lower (below eight years on the Salford Reading Test).

Paired Reading

Paired Reading is a relatively simple educational method which has suddenly become enormously popular. The technique was first described by Morgan (1976) and Morgan and Lyon (1979) but was not immediately taken up on any large scale, possibly because the two journals in which these studies were reported are read by very few teachers.

Interest in Paired Reading among educational psychologists was stimulated by a paper by Bushell *et al.* (1982) presented to the annual course of the Association of Educational Psychologists in 1980. Following the presentation at the course some educational psychologists encouraged schools to work this way. A recent paper by Topping and McKnight (1984) listed ten evaluation studies plus their own.

Paired Reading is based upon a specific technique which is learned by the parent and child, under the guidance of the teacher or psychologist. First, the parent and child learn 'simultaneous reading' – the child and parent read together a book, chosen by the child, in synchrony. The parent adjusts his or her rate of reading to match that of the child. By this process, often supplemented by finger-pointing, the child is aided to read all the words in the passage. The parent is encouraged, or taught if necessary, to praise the child. If the child makes an error, or hesitates for four or five seconds, the parent says the word correctly, the child repeats this, and they then continue in synchrony once more.

In the second phase 'independent reading' the child gradually takes control of the reading process. As confidence increases the child learns to make a sign, perhaps a knock on the table, to indicate that the parent should stop. The child then reads alone. If a word is encountered which the child does not know, the sign can again be given and the parent joins in again with simultaneous reading. Alternatively, if the child makes no sign, but hesitates for about four or five seconds, the parent can give the correct word, and simultaneous reading starts.

In most schemes, a group of parents and children are gathered together, usually at school in an evening, and taught simultaneous reading skills. They practise this under supervision and then put it into operation at home for a week or so. During this time a tutor may visit to check on performance. Independent reading will be taught at a second meeting, and the process repeated. Projects often last for about six to eight weeks and end with a final meeting to report on progress.

The rationale for Paired Reading argues that many poor readers have built up resistance and anxiety. Often the parents have built up similar feelings and may become frustrated with their child's faltering and mistakes and lose their tempers. Paired Reading is designed to help by several methods. It structures the reading process to remove failure. Using simultaneous reading the child will read all words, even if some are 'read' only as a result of copying the parent. Under independent reading any error is quickly corrected and there are no obvious indications of failure. It provides positive feedback as parents are encouraged to praise the child. It removes negative feedback: parents are 'banned' from saying words like 'no' or 'that's wrong', and encouraged to use positive or neutral responses. The process provides a good model for the child. This applies both to the specific aspect of reading, and to a generalized model of the parent as a reader. By developing continuous reading, the child is able to draw upon contextual cues which in turn improves the likelihood of accurate reading.

The feedback from parents and children who have engaged in

Paired Reading is almost always positive. Parents will often report that they had previously stopped hearing their child read, or perhaps had never done so. Paired Reading projects have helped them relax as much as the child, and they often report noticing an improvement in the child's reading.

There has now been a large number of small scale projects which generally show that Paired Reading produces substantial gains in scores on reading tests, often using the Neale Analysis of Reading Ability which produces age-equivalent scores for accuracy, comprehension and rate of reading.

Morgan and Lyon (1979) studied four children whose ages ranged from 8 years 3 months to 11 years 1 month, but whose Neale accuracy scores were between seven months and 3 years 8 months behind their chronological age. They were involved in paired reading for 12 to 13 weeks. The gains in reading age ranged from nine months to 19 months (accuracy) and 10 months to 13 months (comprehension). The mean increases were 11.75 months (accuracy) and 11.5 months (comprehension) in the mean time of 6.25 months.

A study by Bushell *et al.* (1982) took 22 children whose mean age was 10 years 1 month. Their intervention was shorter, with the children receiving practice for about three-quarters of the time reported by Morgan and Lyon, but the children's mean increase in reading, as measured by the Neale, was 5.8 months (accuracy) and 13 months (comprehension).

These early studies suggested that Paired Reading could be effective. Topping and McKnight (1984) have summarized the results of 11 studies, including that of Bushell *et al.* and their results confirm this. These studies covered children from 7 to 13 years of age and included children designated dyslexic, and others of Asian origin. Topping and McKnight analyse the results by comparing the actual gains made with the gains predicted on the assumption that scores on a reading test will increase by one month per calendar month. By this analysis, the actual increases reported range from 1.75 to 9 times those expected.

Overall, these findings are most encouraging. Parents and children generally are happy with the procedures, the children make significant gains in reading ability, and attitudes also improve. Also of note is the fact that comprehension increases. Given these results it is perhaps not surprising that the technique has become so popular; in late 1984 the first National Paired Reading Conference was heavily oversubscribed.

Comments on Paired Reading

Despite such a positive picture, there are issues that require further examination. Most of the projects reported are simple in design. Control groups are not used, since the children act as their own controls. This does not invalidate the results, but it raises the question of whether it is the Paired Reading technique which is important. There are also doubts about the measures used. Apart from Morgan and Lyon's study recent projects have lasted only two or three months (exceptions being those by Jungnitz *et al.*, 1983 and Young and Tyre, 1983). The sensitivity of any standardized reading tests to such short time intervals is doubtful. The most commonly used test, the Neale Analysis of Reading Ability is old (original publication 1958), and its parallel forms can produce discrepant results. The comprehension score is susceptible to serious variation as a result of the construction of the test; only when children score fewer than a specified number of errors on a passage can they then be given the comprehension questions; consequently an improvement of only one or two points for accuracy may lead to the child, on the second testing, answering questions which were not asked on the first occasion. This could lead to an increase in comprehension score of up to seven months when the accuracy score increased by only two months.

Finally, it is important to remember the intervention period has usually been very short. Other studies of remedial reading have shown short term gains are common, but these can be 'washed out' if the children are followed up after one or two years (e.g. Cashdan and Pumfrey, 1969; Cashdan *et al.*, 1971).

There are, therefore, some caveats to the generally positive results for Paired Reading. The evidence can best be summarized at present as showing that the intervention process leads to gains in reading ability in the short term, that it can improve motivation of parents as well as children, but that the durability of these improvements needs further examination.

Further Developments

This section considers two different developments: variations on the Paired Reading scheme, and more complex forms of structured parental involvement.

An aim of Paired Reading is the reduction in anxiety and sense of failure that poor readers often suffer. However, examination of the *total* approach suggests that other factors could be of importance. Paired Reading projects are often presented in a way which is geared to reduce anxiety and failure, and to boost confidence, involvement, motivation and self-esteem. Some projects have had a central aim of ensuring everyone is relaxed. Parents and children would be given drinks and biscuits, the sessions would be light-hearted, and role-plays would demonstrate, in a humorous fashion, how not to hear your child read. To an observer of such sessions, the reduction in anxiety is very plain. Parents will spontaneously reveal that they had fallen into bad habits, did lose their tempers and were annoyed and frustrated. Often children will make similar comments.

Such observations led one to question whether these factors were as important as the Paired Reading technique itself. Accordingly, a study was carried out by a psychologist, Alison Evans, which compared Paired Reading with Relaxed Reading (see Lindsay *et al.*, 1985). The sample comprised 20 children from one middle school, mean age 9 years 4 months, range 8 years 7 months to 10 years 4 months. The children were divided into two main groups. The first was given Paired Reading in the way described above. The parents and children attended three sessions in school: the first to learn and practise simultaneous reading, the second for independent reading, and the final session was held at the end of the project, which lasted six weeks. During this period half the group were visited weekly at home while the other parents were phoned weekly. Both contacts enabled a general check to be kept and support to be given, but the main purpose of the visit to the first group was to check on the correctness of the Paired Reading method.

The Relaxed Reading group was also brought together on three occasions, but Paired Reading techniques were not taught. Instead the emphasis was on showing how listening to children read can go wrong, and how this can be avoided, boosting self-confidence and reducing anxiety. The parents were encouraged to listen to their children, to correct errors gently, not to be critical or upset and generally to be calm. Good models were provided during role play by Alison Evans and a teacher. During the six weeks of the project half the parents were visited while the other five were phoned. The design allowed for examination of the need for Paired Reading per se, and also of the home-visiting model of monitoring.

Analysis of the results showed that both Paired and Relaxed

Reading groups made good progress in reading. The mean rate of increase in reading age per month was 6.5 months accuracy and 8.1 months comprehension for the Paired Reading group; 4.9 months accuracy and 9.1 months comprehension for the Relaxed Reading group. In all cases the rates of gains were significantly greater than those to be expected on the basis of the children's rate of improvement in reading prior to the intervention. These results, therefore, confirmed the other findings for Paired Reading's effectiveness, but also showed that Relaxed Reading could be effective.

A comparison was therefore made of the four conditions: Paired Reading with and without home visiting, and Relaxed Reading with and without home visiting. The result suggested that Relaxed Reading was as effective as Paired Reading, i.e. a simplified form of intervention – without the need for teaching parents and children the specific techniques of Paired Reading but helping them to be more positive – can be equally effective. Also, this does not require the time-consuming home visiting necessary to check on the correct application of the technique.

'Shared Reading' was developed by the Cleveland Psychological Service and Learning Support Service (Greening and Spenceley, 1984a). It is based upon the Simultaneous Reading stage of Paired Reading but Greening and Spenceley claim that its theoretical base is different: 'the emphasis is much more on "sharing" than "pairing"' (Greening and Spenceley, 1984b, p.10). They argue that because the technique is simpler, it is easier to acquire by parents and so needs fewer teaching sessions for parents and children. Also it can be used with younger children and those with lower reading ages.

They provide some data on a project with ten children aged 5 years 3 months to 7 years. The Salford reading test was administered before and after the project which lasted five weeks. Only five children scored on the reading test before this project, and their mean gain was 9.4 months during this five-week period. No data are presented for the other five children. Greening and Spenceley report that the children's reading strategies improved from a word by word approach to reading sentences for sense.

Scott and Ballard (1983) report a study of four 11- to 12-year-old children, all with marked difficulties in reading, where both parents and teachers were trained to modify their responses to the children's errors, using a technique reported by McNaughton and Glynn (1981).

The parents and teachers were taught to increase their delay before correcting an error, provide more praise and give more prompts. The parents' and teachers' skills on these criteria were examined before and after training and it was found, for example, that parents initially gave little praise and corrected their children too soon. However, they could be trained to alter this behaviour, and the study showed that this was maintained three months after the project. The children's reading ability was measured pre- and post-project on a variety of measures derived from work in New Zealand. The general finding was of an increase in reading ability of about two to four years of reading age during a period of nine months.

This study is interesting as it brings together teachers and parents in the same instructional programme. Also, a major aim is to increase praise for correct responses. But unlike Paired Reading the children are encouraged to read alone.

Conclusions

It is apparent that the involvement of parents in the development of their children's reading can be highly beneficial. The studies surveyed vary greatly from just encouraging parents to hear their children read, to attempts to give parents specific teaching techniques.

There seems to be good evidence that simple parent involvement projects such as those in Haringey and Belfield can be organized by schools, and are popular with parents and children. Paired Reading, a specific teaching approach, has also been shown to be popular and to produce gains in reading ability. Comparison with the simpler approaches is difficult as Paired Reading projects have usually lasted a matter of weeks (normally six to eight weeks) while the Belfield project, for example, has involved the same children for about three years. Thus, although the gains for Paired Reading projects in terms of rate of improvement per month seem far more impressive, the long-term effects are unknown. It is hoped that a series of studies by Topping, a psychologist in Kirklees, will produce evidence on this.

Other studies have shown that parents can be taught to use teaching techniques which may be regarded as specialized – indeed some are not even common among teachers in primary schools; Scott and Ballard (1983), for example, have successfully taught parents the skills of error correction.

On the other hand, the study of Relaxed Reading has shown that a simple, easy to organize project can produce gains in reading performance which match those achieved by the more complex schemes. In terms of cost effectiveness an approach such as Relaxed Reading would appear to be a choice worth considering.

However, this is perhaps too simple an analysis. The studies surveyed have included a wide variety of children with different needs. For many it appears that a relatively simple parent involvement approach may be enough. This may be helped or highlighted, particularly at the junior school level, by a short-term specific course of Relaxed Reading. The emphasis on making the reading process relaxed and non-anxiety provoking may be particularly beneficial. For some children there may be the need to use more specialized techniques; for some parents, the added structure of such techniques may be beneficial. The use of home visiting needs to be considered, since this is very costly in terms of professionals' time. The involvement of students (e.g. Lindsay *et al.* (1985), Belcher (1984)) can help, but usually only for initial short projects. Once a system is underway the school would need to rely on its own resources. Some parents clearly enjoy and welcome this component (e.g. Sigston *et al.*, 1984), but the cost-effectiveness and practicality aspects must be considered. Also, initial evidence from Topping's work suggests that home visiting may not be required, even with Paired Reading (personal communication).

Schools vary in the extent to which they are prepared to become involved in parental involvement schemes. A study of 16 infant and first schools by Hannon and Cuckle (1984) showed that the heads and teachers supported parental involvement in reading in principle, but not parents hearing their children read at home. The involvement of parents in the development of their children's reading is important, and schools can hardly be unaware that it happens anyway for some parents.

The projects reviewed suggest a range of opportunities for teachers and parents to work together in partnership to meet the needs of the individual child, and offer a way of helping all parents to offer the support that some children receive. It seems likely that parents from ethnic minority groups are among those who are least certain in offering such support, and may gain from a structured involvement in partnership with teachers. Reading is an obvious area to tackle since there is considerable experience to build on – however there is no reason why similar schemes could not then be considered for number or spelling or other areas of the core curriculum.

CHAPTER 10
Overview

Certain themes are common to every approach mentioned. These include the need for careful planning and recording whether by an individual teacher or a school. In general this is a daunting task for a single teacher starting a new approach, and it is not difficult to overlook some aspect that is missing, or some way of making an approach much easier and more cost-effective, so team approaches are probably easier as well as more interesting. It is also much easier to see whether things work well, to evaluate their effectiveness if more than one teacher is involved, or perhaps if two similar approaches can be compared. It may also be useful to involve the available time and experience outside the school – a visiting teaching service, a psychologist, an adviser or inspector.

The role of parents as partners is also common – whether directly involved in provision for a child's needs, or in being made aware of problems. It is likely that involving parents when children have an identified problem will be easier if there is already an ethos in a school that promotes easy interaction between school and families. Parents whose confidence in talking to teachers or visiting schools needs active encouragement, and parents from some ethnic minority groups, are likely to need this and some planning to ensure that language is not a barrier to communication. While their children should not be excluded from provision to help with special needs, some of the identification procedures should be used with care. This is of course true of all children; it is self-evidently pointless to worry parents or others until one is clear that there is a problem. However, for ethnic minority groups, norm-referenced or standardized tests are inappropriate as the sole evidence to back up a problem, and it is particularly important to collect evidence of trying to change behaviour or teach missing skills. It is also helpful to check that what the school sees as a problem is similarly viewed by the parents rather than assuming it must be.

The approaches described will not be seen as compatible by some teachers and psychologists. Since they all have some evidence of effectiveness, and none is so comprehensive that it meets all requirements, it seems rather pedantic to object that they derive from models which can be seen as conflicting. It is probably less the case that models conflict than that individuals who espouse or reject a model conflict with each other. Behavioural approaches in particular appear to attract adherents who reject any other models, and a complementary group who refuse to use such approaches. When looking for ways to help children with special needs this sort of attitude seems inappropriate. Some of the ways of helping individuals with inappropriate behaviour or with learning difficulties derived from applied behavioural approaches are quick, effective and easy to use. To reject them without trying them is difficult to justify.

Using an early identification procedure will provide a check to supplement teacher observation and impression, will offer a broader comparison with children of the same age and may identify problems that were not noticed. This may complement the use of an assessment through teaching approach which could follow it. It seems very important that teachers should have a menu of possible approaches and the freedom to select ones that seem relevant, useful, practicable and compatible with their style. Similarly, schools vary in their number of children with special needs and the ways in which they are organized, and different approaches are appropriate for different schools.

Whatever approaches schools adopt it is helpful to review these and to attempt to see how useful they are. For many schools even a meeting to review approaches to special needs would be an innovation. Others may wish alone or in conjunction with a psychologist to decide some targets and check whether these are reached. Whether a school already has a policy that might be reviewed, or is working towards one, a regular examination of efficiency is helpful. While the emphasis has been on the teacher and the school, in many areas groups of schools meet and comparing approaches can be informative.

Of course one cannot fail to recognize that at present schools and teachers are under stress. Resources and money are or seem scarce; teachers' action is a limitation on developments for significant periods. Many demands are emanating from central government,

Her Majesty's Inspectorate, LEAs and others. There are probably at least as many suggestions for change and new initiatives now as at any other period. Catering for the full range of children with special needs is only one. It is a very important one – so important that it is backed by legislation. It is also one that has a lot of potential positive outcomes, for the recipients and their families and thus for society at large, but also for other children and for teachers and schools. Plans for children with special needs often have implications for other planning and teaching, and can make classrooms easier, more pleasant and more effective if all children are working to some purpose. Primary schools have a long tradition of helping children with problems; now a range of approaches to help them in this role is emerging at a time when there is considerable enthusiasm for development. The 1981 Education Act, however cumbersome, is legislation that derives from what the Warnock Report described as good practice, and its intention to encourage this in all schools has wide support.

The problem solving approach outlined in Chapter 3 and referred to throughout subsequent chapters offers teachers and schools a framework that is flexible and adaptable. It can accommodate any of the procedures or techniques outlined, and any others that teachers already use or encounter on courses, in reading or from visits. Indeed it can be a useful framework for other concerns although its use for developments in special needs has been emphasized.

As we said in our Preface, we are excited and optimistic about the philosophy of the Warnock Report and the 1981 Education Act. Even the Act, despite its limitations, has an implicit vision of a better educational system, a better deal for all children with special needs and their families. The challenge to schools and to individual teachers may be difficult but it is also exciting. We hope that this book has offered some constructive help in meeting the challenge and translating philosophy into practical reality.

References

ACKERMAN, T., GUNETT, D., KENWARD, P., LEADBETTER, P., MASON, L., MATHEW, C. and WINTERINGHAM, G. (1983). *DATAPAC: An Interim Report*. Unpublished.

ADVISORY CENTRE FOR EDUCATION (1983). *ACE Special Education Handbook*. London: ACE.

AINSCOW, M. and MUNCEY, J. (1981) *Tutor's Guide: SNAP Learning Difficulties Course*. Coventry Education Department.

AINSCOW, M. and MUNCEY, J. (1984). *SNAP*. Cardiff: Drake Educational Associates.

BELCHER, M. (1984). 'Parents can be a major asset in teaching reading', *Remedial Education*, 19, 162–164.

BOOKBINDER, G. (1976). *The Salford Sentence Reading Test*. London: Hodder and Stoughton.

BULLOCK REPORT. GREAT BRITAIN, DEPARTMENT OF EDUCATION AND SCIENCE (1975). *A Language for Life*. London: HMSO.

BUSHELL, R., MILLER, A. and ROBSON, D. (1982). 'Parents as remedial teachers', *Association of Educational Psychologists Journal*, 5, 9, 7–13.

CARNINE, D. and GILBERT, J. (1979). *Direct Instruction Reading*. Ohio: Merrill.

CASHDAN, A. and PUMFREY, P. (1969). 'Some effects of the remedial teaching of reading', *Educational Research*, 11, 138–142.

CASHDAN, A., PUMFREY, P. and LUNZER, E. (1971). 'Children receiving remedial teaching in reading', *Educational Research*, 13, 98–105.

CORNWALL, K. and SPICER, J. (1982). DECP enquiry: the role of the educational psychologist in the discovery and assessment of children requiring special education', *Occasional Papers of Division of Educational and Child Psychology*, 6, 2, 3–30.

COX, C.B. and BOYSON, R. (1975). *Black Paper 1975*. London: J.M. Dent and Sons.

DAVIE, R., BUTLER, N. and GOLDSTEIN, H. (1972). *From Birth to Seven.* London: Longman.

DELECCO, J.R. and CRAWFORD, W.R. (1974). *The Psychology of Learning and Instruction* (2nd Edition). Englewood Cliffs, New Jersey: Prentice-Hall.

DOUGLAS, J.W.B. (1964). *The Home and the School.* London MacGibbon and Key.

ENGLEMANN, S. and CARNINE, D. (1982). *Theory of Instruction: Principles and Applications.* Ohio: Merrill.

FISH REPORT. INNER LONDON EDUCATION AUTHORITY (1985). *Educational Opportunities for All.* London: ILEA.

FORMENTIN, T. and CSAPO, M. (1980). *Precision Teaching.* Vancouver: Centre for Human Development and Research

GARDNER, W.I. (1977) *Learning and Behaviour Characteristics of Exceptional Children and Youth.* Boston: Allyn and Bacon.

GIPPS, C. and GROSS, H. (1984). *Local Education Authority Policies in Identification and Provision for Children with Special Educational Needs in Ordinary Schools.* University of London Institute of Education: Screening and Special Education Provision – Schools Project. Occasional Paper No. 3.

GREAT BRITAIN. DEPARTMENT OF EDUCATION AND SCIENCE (1975). *Circular 2/75: The discovery of children requiring special education and the assessment of their needs.* London: DES.

GREAT BRITAIN. DEPARTMENT OF EDUCATION AND SCIENCE (1980). *Special Needs in Education.* London: DES.

GREAT BRITAIN, DEPARTMENT OF EDUCATION AND SCIENCE (1981). *Circular 8/81: Education Act 1981.* London: DES.

GREAT BRITAIN. DEPARTMENT OF EDUCATION AND SCIENCE (1983). *Circular 1/83: Assessments and statements of special educational needs.* London: DES.

GREAT BRITAIN. MINISTRY OF EDUCATION (1946). *Pamphlet No. 5: Special Educational Treatment.* London: HMSO.

GREENING, M. and SPENCELEY, J. (1984a). *Shared Reading: Teachers' Manual.* Cleveland County Council Education Department.

GREENING, M. and SPENCELEY, J. (1984b). 'Shared Reading: A review of the Cleveland project'. Cleveland County Psychological Service: *In Psych.,* 11, 2, 10–13.

GRONLUND, N.E. (1970). *Stating Behavioural Objectives for Classroom Instruction* (2nd Edition). Englewood Cliffs: Prentice-Hall.

HANNON, P. and CUCKLE, P. (1984). 'Involving parents in the teaching of reading: A study of current school practice', *Educational Research,* 26, 7–13.

HANNON, P., JACKSON, A. and PAGE, B. (1985). 'Implementation and take-up of a project to involve parents in the teaching of reading'. In: TOPPING, K. and WOLFENDALE, S. (Eds) *Parental Involvement in Children's Reading.* London: Croom Helm.

HANNON, P., LONG, R. and WHITEHURST, L. (1984). Parental involvement in early childhood education: some current research. *SERCH* (Sheffield Educational Research Current Highlights), 6, 1–5. Sheffield University, Division of Education.

HARGREAVES, D., HESTER, S. and MELLOR, F. (1975). *Deviance in Classrooms.* London: Routledge and Kegan Paul.

HEWISON, J. and TIZARD, J. (1980). 'Parental involvement and reading attainment', *British Journal of Educational Psychology,* 50, 209–215.

HOWARTH, C.I. (1980). 'The structure of effective psychology: man as a problem-solver'. In: CHAPMAN, A.J. and JONES, D.M. (Eds) *Models of Man.* Leicester: British Psychological Society.

JACKSON, A. and HANNON, P. (1981). *The Belfield Reading Project.* Rochdale: Belfield Community Council.

JUNGNITZ, G., OLIVE, S. and TOPPING, K. (1983). 'The development and evaluation of a paired reading project', *Journal of Community Education.* 2, 4, 14–22.

KEOGH, B.K. (1982). 'Children's temperament and teachers' decisions'. In: Ciba Foundation Symposium 89. *Temperamental Differences in Infants and Young Children.* London: Pitman.

KNEEDLER, R.D. and TARVER, S.G. (1977). *Changing Perspectives in Special Education.* Ohio: Merrill.

KOUNIN, J.S. (1970). *Discipline and Group Management in Classrooms.* New York: R.E. Kreiger.

LINDSAY, G. (1974). Early identification of learning difficulties. Unpublished M.Ed. (Ed. Psych.) thesis, University of Birmingham.

LINDSAY, G. (1979a). The Infant Rating Scale: Some evidence on its validity from a selected sample of children', *Occasional Papers of the Division of Educational and Child Psychology,* 3, 2, 27–41. British Psychological Society.

LINDSAY, G. (1979b). The early identification of learning difficulties and the monitoring of children's progress. Unpublished doctoral thesis, University of Birmingham.

LINDSAY, G. (1981). *The Infant Rating Scale.* Sevenoaks: Hodder and Stoughton.

LINDSAY, G., EVANS, A. and JONES, B. (1985). 'Paired Reading versus Relaxed Reading: A comparison', *British Journal of Educational Psychology,* 55, 304–309.

LINDSAY, G. and WEDELL, K. (1982). 'The early identification of educationally "at risk" children revisited,' *Journal of Learning Disabilities,* 15, 212–217.

MCNAUGHTON, S. and GLYNN, T. (1981). 'Delayed versus immediate attention to oral reading errors: Effects on accuracy and self-correction', *Educational Psychology*, 33, 57–65.

MAGER, R.F. (1972). *Preparing Instructional Objectives*. New York: Fearan Publications.

MAGGS, A., MCMILLAN, K., PATCHING, W. and HAWKE, H. (1981). 'Accelerating spelling skills using morphographs', *Educational Psychology*, 1, 49–56.

MORGAN, R. (1976). 'Paired Reading tuition: a preliminary report on a technique for cases of reading deficit', *Child: Care, Health and Development*, 2, 13–28.

MORGAN, R. and LYON, E. (1979). 'Paired Reading – A preliminary report on a technique for parental tuition of reading-retarded children', *Journal of Child Psychology and Psychiatry*, 20, 151–160.

NATIONAL FOUNDATION FOR RESEARCH INTO CRIPPLING DISEASES (1976). *Integrating the Disabled*. (Report of the Snowdon Working Party.) London: NFRCD.

PEARSON, L. (1980). 'The assessment of learning difficulties', *Remedial Education*, 15, 3, 124–129.

PEARSON, L. (1985). *Survey of Educational Psychological Services and the 1981 Education Act*. National Association of Principal Educational Psychologists. (available from LEA Psychological Services).

PEARSON, L. and HOWARTH, I. (1982). 'Training professional psychologists', *Bulletin of the British Psychological Society*, 35, 375–6.

PEARSON, L. and QUINN, J. (1986). *The Bury Infant Check*. Windsor: NFER-NELSON.

PEARSON, L. and TWEDDLE, D. (1984). 'The formulation and use of behavioural objectives'. In: FONTANA, D. (Ed) *Behaviourism and Learning Theory in Education*. Edinburgh: Scottish Academic Press in association with the British Psychological Society.

PINNEY, F.J. (1984). A comparative evaluation of two language programmes: DISTAR Language 1 and GRIP. Unpublished M.Ed. thesis, University of Birmingham.

PLOWDEN REPORT. GREAT BRITAIN. DEPARTMENT OF EDUCATION AND SCIENCE CENTRAL ADVISORY COUNCIL FOR EDUCATION (ENGLAND) (1967). *Children and their Primary Schools*, London: HMSO.

PUMFREY, P.D., (1977). *Measuring reading abilities*. London: Hodder and Stoughton.

ROBERTSON, J. (1981). *Effective Classroom Control*. London: Hodder and Stoughton.

RODGERS, B. (1984). 'The trend of reading standards re-assessed', *Educational Research*, 26, 153–166.

SATZ, P. and FLETCHER, J. (1979). 'Early screening tests: some uses and abuses', *Journal of Learning Disabilities*, 12, 1, 56–59.

SCOTT, J.M. and BALLARD, K. (1983). 'Training parents and teachers in remedial reading procedures for children with learning difficulties', *Educational Psychology*, 3, 15–30.

SIGSTON, A., ADDINGTON, J., BANKS, V. and STRIESOW, M. (1984). 'Progress with parents: An account and evaluation of a home reading project for poor readers', *Remedial Education*, 19, 170–173.

SMITH, H. and MARSH, M. (n.d.). *Have You a Minute? The Fox Hill Reading Project*. Available from Fox Hill First School, Sheffield.

START, K. and WELLS, B. (1972). *The Trend of Reading Standards*. Windsor: NFER.

SWANN REPORT. GREAT BRITAIN, DEPARTMENT OF EDUCATION AND SCIENCE (1985). *Education for All*. London: HMSO. (Also available as a short summary document under the same title.)

TIZARD, J., SCHOFIELD, W.N. and HEWISON, J. (1982). 'Collaboration between teachers and parents in assisting children's reading', *British Journal of Educational Psychology*, 52, 1–15.

TOPPING, K. and MCKNIGHT, G. (1984). 'Paired Reading – and parent power', *Special Education: Forward Trends*, 11, 3, 12–14.

WARNOCK REPORT. GREAT BRITAIN. DEPARTMENT OF EDUCATION AND SCIENCE (1978). *Special Education Needs*. London: HMSO.

WEINBERGER, J. (1983). *The Fox Hill Reading Workshop*. London: Family Service Unit Publication.

WESTMACOTT, E.V.S. and CAMERON, R.J. (1981) *Behaviour Can Change*. Basingstoke: Globe Education.

WHELDALL, K. and MERRETT, F. (1984). *Positive Teaching: The Behavioural Approach*. London: George Allen and Unwin.

WHITE, D.R. and HARING, N.G. (1980). *Exceptional Children*. Ohio: Merrill.

WILLIAMS, H., MUNCEY, J., WINTERINGHAM, D. and DUFFY, M. (1980). *Precision Teaching: A Classroom Manual*. Coventry: Coventry Education Department.

WOLFENDALE, S. and BRYANS, T. (1979). *Identification of Learning Difficulties: A Model for Intervention*. National Association for Remedial Education.

YOUNG, P. and TYRE, C. (1983). *Dyslexia or Illiteracy?* Milton Keynes: Open University Press.